Forward

These terms were compiled with a significant amount of blood, sweat, and tears—sometimes literally. While extramarital affairs, adoptions, and 'donor-conception' through a more traditional means have been around almost as long as humans, it is the rise in popularity of genealogy, individualism, and inexpensive direct-to-consumer (DTC) DNA tests that has fostered a new community and awareness. There's still much we don't understand about DNA, genetics, and epigenetics, including their influence on our health, personality traits, preferences, abilities, and behaviors. We possess an innate biological desire to know where we come from, what makes us tick, and who our ancestors are.

One thing we do know is that children possess an immense capacity for love and can intuitively feel when they're being raised in a family where they're not genetically related to one or both parents. The separation from our genetic parents inflicts a primal wound that cannot be merely fixed by substituting one set of parents for another. We know the difference.

The impact of this trauma varies widely among individuals, ranging from minimal to life-long challenges. By acknowledging this wound, however, we can begin to heal it. It is in the child's best interest to know from birth who their genetic parents are if they're different from the parents raising them. No one should ever have to learn from an email because a lederhosen commercial drew them in, that they are not who they thought they were.

In January 2018 I woke up and checked my email like most of us do. Little did I know, this would radically alter how I saw myself, my sense of family, where I thought I belonged in the world, and change the direction of my life. I was raised by a single mother. My father was a heroin addict and wasn't present in my childhood but I often spent time with my grandparents. I was just dark enough to be half Black. This was my narrative. We had traced our ancestry back to three slave brothers sold in Texas and I wanted to know where in Africa we came from.

By my late 20s my dad had cleaned himself up and we had reconciled. He agreed to a DTC DNA to solve the mystery of which part of Africa we came from. Neither of us expected the results to show I wasn't related to him and that I was half Jewish.

The moment I opened that email, I knew my dad couldn't be my genetic dad because I had zero African DNA. My world stopped spinning in that instant. Staring back at me from the mirror was now a stranger. It took more than six months for me to identify my genetic father, most of my family were deceased or didn't want contact. I felt isolated with my identity crisis, grief, and shame and my sense of belonging was turned inside out. I mean, who grows up thinking their one thing only to discover their something else? It turns out I am not alone.

Motivated by my experience and a lack of information about DNA surprises (or misattributed parentage experiences (MPE)) as well as resources for people who have this life-changing discovery, and lack of rights to my identity and accurate records, I co-founded Right to Know in 2019. This non-profit organization is committed to supporting everyone affected by genetic identity issues and the disruption of genetic continuity due to adoption, assisted reproduction, or non-paternal events (NPE). Right to Know promotes understanding of the complex intersection of genetic information, identity, and family dynamics through education, support, and advocacy. We estimate that 1 in 20 people have misattributed parentage from an undisclosed donor conception, adoption, or NPE, that's more than 16 million Americans.

Discussing a subject becomes challenging without a common vocabulary. Each community or profession develops its own lexicon and acronyms over time, which evolve as our understanding deepens. We don't even have a name for the broad community of people who are impacted by the loss of genetic continuity—this includes children (not just young people, but adult offspring), parents, and other relatives.

These communities—adoption, assisted reproduction, and NPEs—share many overlapping similarities with some distinct differences (visit www.RightToKnow.us for more on this). Some individuals grow up aware of their adoption, donor conception, or the existence of a different genetic father out there, while others are taken by surprise; but regardless of the circumstances, the loss of genetic continuity affects us all.

Through years of dialogue with thousands impacted by adoption, assisted reproduction, and NPEs, along with extensive research, I've developed a glossary to facilitate conversations about genetic continuity loss and identity. I have read countless books, articles, and studies; attended conferences; and talked to specialists in related fields on the topics of adoption, assisted reproduction, identity, therapy, trauma, communication, legal rights, ethnicity, and belonging. It is through my six years of research, interviews, and firsthand experience that I developed this list of terms and definitions. This list is intended to provide the words needed for people impacted by loss of genetic continuity to talk about what they are experiencing. It also aims to generate much needed societal conversations about genetic identity and family.

By framing these concepts within the context of movies, I aim to bridge the gap between complex genetic identity issues and family dynamics with universally understood narratives. Films, with their rich storytelling and emotional depth, offer a relatable and accessible medium to explore and visualize these intricate themes. This approach not only aids in the comprehension of these terms but also resonates on a personal level, allowing readers to see reflections of their own experiences in the familiar scenarios of cinema.

This glossary represents the current consensus within this emerging community and its diverse members. Not everyone may agree with every definition, as opinions vary greatly depending on one's perspective, whether as a genetic parent, a child, or a raising parent or an adoptee, DCP, or someone with an NPE. As research advances, these definitions will undoubtedly evolve, but this serves as a good place to start.

Kara

P.S. Give grace to others and especially to yourself.

Terms

𝒜
adoptee

...is someone who is legally taken into a family, often not their genetic family, and is raised as a member of that family.

In "The Labyrinth of Life," an adoptee traverses a complex, maze-like world, echoing their intricate journey through adoption. The labyrinth symbolizes their path of self-discovery, filled with puzzles and challenges that reflect the adoptee's experiences of confusion, isolation, and eventual connection. Encountering a range of characters, each embodies different emotions and aspects of the adoptee's journey. This tale is not just about reaching the end of the maze, but understanding one's place within it, capturing the depth and bittersweet reality of seeking origins and forging a unique identity amidst the twists and turns of life.

The Labyrinth of Life (Labyrinth)

1

Adoptees, or 'adoptive person' as some prefer, are separated from their genetic parents and often grapple with a primal wound that impacts mental health and identity development. This wound arises from the absence of genetic mirroring, leading to genetic bewilderment, where the lack of visible familial traits hinders a sense of belonging.

With the sealing of their original birth certificate (OBC) during the adoption process, adoptees face obscured histories. This leaves adoptees with limited access to personal medical history and familial information. This barrier can evoke a deep sense of loss, extending beyond unknown relatives to missing links about personal traits, health predispositions, and behaviors.

Adoptees may feel societal pressure to view adoption as a gift, burdening them with unwarranted gratitude expectations that impact the shaping of their self-esteem. They might internalize feelings of being 'given away', which can lead to lowered self-worth and the belief that they must justify their place in their adoptive family and society.

For late discovery adoptees (LDA), finding out about their adoption as adults can cause an identity crisis. Confronted with a false life narrative, LDAs struggle with betrayal and mourn the loss of their lived history. This can affect their trust in relationships and their sense of self like LDDCP and people with an NPE.

In a society fascinated with genetics, underscored by the booming DTC DNA market, an adoptee's lack of genetic ties can feel isolating. This isolation may be compounded by challenges in forming attachments and accepting personal achievements, as they are often measured against a backdrop of those not related to them. Despite these challenges, many adoptees engage in a journey of self-discovery, seeking to reconcile their origins with their life experiences. This can be both enlightening and arduous, as adoptees strive to weave the disparate threads of their lives into a coherent narrative.

Being an adoptee encompasses a wide spectrum of emotions and experiences. This journey requires strong inner resolve and deep introspection, leading to a profound understanding of one's identity and a heightened sense of belonging. It reflects the indomitable nature of the human spirit. Through this process, adoptees often develop a unique perspective on life and relationships.

𝒜
adoption

...is legally taking another's child and bringing them up as one's own child.

You're living in "The Truman Show," oops... the "True-You Show." This isn't just about discovering a pre-written life script but also confronting the reality of being raised in a world that's not quite what it seems. Like Truman, you navigate through a life where your origins are unknown, and the journey to self-discovery is filled with unexpected turns and hidden truths. Being adopted adds layers to your identity, making your quest for self-realization not just a personal journey, but a need to uncover the deeper narrative of your life. Unraveling your genetic origins often further complicates your search for identity, creating a complex exploration about belonging in and connecting to a world where the only constant is change.

The True-You-Show (The Trueman Show)

3

Separation from genetic parents can cause a primal wound in a child, creating trauma that varies in intensity. Recognizing and addressing this loss at every developmental stage is crucial for minimizing psychological impacts on a child.

Infant adoption is an industry—for every one infant available for adoption, there's 36 families waiting. This imbalance can lead to pressure on some women to relinquish their babies. Organizations like **Saving Our Sisters** provide essential long-term support to families who might only need temporary assistance in order to remain together.

Family preservation should be the paramount objective, wherever feasible. This approach underscores the critical importance of maintaining the child's connection with their genetic family, providing a continuum of care and emotional stability that is vital for their development. It involves a concerted effort to offer comprehensive support to families facing challenges, thereby preventing unnecessary separations. This honors the inherent bond between parent and child but also safeguards the child's psychological and emotional well-being by maintaining their familial and cultural ties. It places the best in interest of the child first, recognizing that a nurturing and secure family environment with accesses to genetic mirroring, medical history information, familial history, and cultural and familial traditions is indispensable for their growth and development.

When removal from genetic parents is necessary, kinship/relative adoption is the preferred option. If that is not possible, guardianship embracing the principles of 'open adoption' stands as the ethical alternative. Guardianship provides the care provider with the right to make legal decisions for the child like a parent but does not sever the child's ties to their genetic family, rename the child, or possibly change the child's birth date and place of birth which can occur in the adoption process.

An open adoption involves ongoing contact between genetic (birth) and raising (adoptive) parents and is beneficial for the child. A Post-Adoption Contact Agreement (PACA) should be used, outlining the nature of contact (such as letters, calls, or visits) and its frequency. PACAs are not legally enforceable in most states, they're considered 'Good Faith Agreements' and can serve as means to

document expectations for post-placement contact. It can be almost impossible for the genetic parents of a child to enforce a PACA even if the courts in a state that enforces such agreements due to barriers in using the legal system such as the cost of an attorney, understanding their rights, etc.

In stepparent adoptions, the new spouse legally adopts their partner's child, often following the relinquishment or death of one genetic parent. It's vital to continually inform the child about their birth parent to preserve their memory. This ongoing dialogue helps the child understand their origins and maintain a connection with their genetic heritage. We need birth certificate reform that would allow the genetic parent to be retained on the document while also acknowledging the new spouse. This change would more accurately reflect the child's familial connections and honor their complete heritage.

We are biologically programmed to seek knowledge about our origins, including physical resemblances and personality traits. A child's desire to understand their genetic identity should not be viewed as a critique of their raising (adoptive) parent(s). Recognizing and honoring a child's right to know about their genetic roots reflects an understanding that this curiosity is a fundamental part of each individual's psychological well-being. Open and honest communication about their genetic heritage nurtures a sense of identity and belonging.

It's always important to consider the child's best interests, and this is exponentially true for international and trans-cultural adoption as it impacts the child's cultural and ethnic identity. Children adopted across international or ethnic lines encounter distinct challenges in reconciling their heritage, identity, and sense of belonging. Such adoptions risk severing ties to their cultural roots, an integral part of their personal identity.

Trans-cultural adoptions should be considered only when all other options are exhausted. When these adoptions do occur, it's critical to afford children ample opportunities to engage with and understand their cultural heritage, fostering a well-rounded and secure sense of self. Adults who grew up in such situations frequently express a sense of perpetual outsider status, feeling disconnected from their birth culture due to a lack of lived experience and from their adoptive culture due to differences in looks and mannerisms.

Types of Adoption

- **Adult adoption**: when someone is adopted after they reach adulthood, age 18. This sometimes occurs after an adoptee (LDDDCP or someone with an NPE) finds their genetic parent(s) and they wish to have their legal birth certificate show their accurate genetic parentage.

- **Closed adoption**: there is no contact and typically no identifying information exchanged between the genetic and raising families, and the records of the adoption are sealed. *A closed adoption should never occur.*

- **Domestic infant adoption (DIA)**: adopting a newborn or very young baby from the same country as the raising (adoptive) parent, rather than internationally.

- **Foster care adoption**: adopting a child who has been placed in the public foster care system, typically due to being removed from their original home for safety or welfare reasons.

- **International adoption**: adopting a child from a different country, which involves complying with the legal requirements of both the child's country of origin and the raising (adoptive) parents' home country. Rarely should children be adopted out of their country of origin.

- **Kinship/relative adoption**: when a child is adopted by someone related to one of child's genetic (birth) parents.

- **Open adoption**: the genetic (birth) and raising (adoptive) families have some form of ongoing contact, which can range from exchanging letters and photos to regular in-person visits. If an open adoption is agreed upon, raising (adoptive) parents should not be allowed to permanently close the adoption later.

- **Stepparent adoption**: the legal process by which a stepparent becomes the legal parent of their spouse's genetic or adoptive child, often erasing the genetic parent's information when a new birth certificate is issued.

- **Trans-racial adoption (TRA)**: A child who is adopted into a family that has a different ethnicity than that of the adoptive family. Children should remain with in their genetic family and if adoption must occur, it should be with a family with the same ethnicity.

𝒜

ambiguous loss

...is a psychological term that refers to a loss that occurs without closure or clear understanding.

Picture your life as a subplot in "Back to the Future", but instead of Marty worrying about his parents' prom date, you're navigating your search for genetic family. This sends you through your own historical timeline. Each page turned is like fading in and out of the photograph - connections appear and disappear, leaving you with more questions than a paradox in a time loop. In this version, the DeLorean can't take you back to meet these characters or fill in the blanks of your story. Instead the DeLorean brings you random information about the past. You're left piecing together a family puzzle where some pieces will forever be missing in time.

Back to the Fading Past (Back to the Future)

Ambiguous loss occurs when emotional closure is difficult or not possible given a lack of available information. It can feel like a never-ending trauma because you cannot have a complete picture. There are two primary forms:

1. **Physical Absence with Psychological Presence.** This happens when a loved one is physically absent but remains in the minds and hearts of those left behind. Examples include missing persons or an estranged child/parent.

2. **Psychological Absence with Physical Presence:** This occurs when a person is physically present but psychologically or emotionally unavailable or changed. E.g. in cases of severe mental illness, addiction, brain injuries, or Alzheimer's.

When applied to someone who's had a DNA surprise or is searching for genetic relatives, this type of loss can occur from: the discovery of genetic relatives who are deceased (physical absence with psychological presence) or the realization that known family members are not genetically related to you or your new living genetic relatives that you know little about and don't have previous shared experiences with (psychological absence with physical presence).

Discovery of Unknown Relations: Learning about new family members introduces a sense of loss for relationships and connections that were never known or experienced, yet now hold a significant part in one's life story.

Altered Family Dynamics: Discovering that a close family member is not genetically related can lead to a feeling of psychological absence, where the emotional and psychological understanding of these relationships is transformed, despite their ongoing physical presence.

Identity Reassessment: This type of ambiguous loss often triggers a profound reassessment of personal identity, heritage, and familial bonds, as individuals grapple with integrating new, often unexpected, information into their understanding of who they are and where they come from.

Unresolved Grief: Ambiguous loss can be marked by unresolved grief and a lack of closure, stemming from unanswered questions and the challenge of reconciling newfound knowledge that may not be a complete picture with existing beliefs about oneself and one's family.

_A_

assisted reproduction

...is a method of conception other than sexual intercourse.

Picture this: you're in "Ocean's Conception: The Great Sperm Bank Heist", where the plan is to create life, but not in the way you'd expect. Instead of a dashing George Clooney planning a casino robbery, you've got a team of doctors and scientists orchestrating the ultimate creation caper. The mission? To bypass traditional reproduction with high-tech tactics, a bit of lab magic, and a whole lot of planning. It's a strategic operation where a baby, more precious than gold, is the end goal, and the "casino" is a fertility clinic. Just when you think you know the game, the plot takes a turn, and you realize the house always has a surprise or two up its sleeve. Then you remember you're making a human life and you proceed with caution.

Ocean's Conception: The Great Sperm Bank Heist
(Ocean's 11)

9

The first recorded case of artificial insemination by donor occurred in 1884 when Dr. William Pancoast, in a highly unethical act, used sperm from the 'best looking' medical student in the class to inseminate a woman under anesthesia without her knowledge but with the consent of her husband. This act, which the woman learned of only years later, opened the door to the concept of sperm donor insemination.

Historically, the Catholic Church and societal norms viewed artificial insemination as akin to infidelity, raising ethical and moral concerns. Over time, however, as science advanced and societal views evolved, assisted reproduction technologies (ARTs) became more accepted and sophisticated. This evolution led to the development of various technologies including in vitro fertilization (IVF), use of donor sperm and eggs, embryo donation, and surrogacy.

IVF, a significant breakthrough in ART, was first successfully achieved with the birth of Louise Brown in 1978. This development marked a turning point in fertility treatments, offering hope to countless individuals and couples facing infertility challenges. The advent of egg donation in the 1980s further expanded the possibilities, aiding women with low ovarian reserve or poor egg quality.

The focus in assisted reproduction has been on providing people with a baby with little concern for the rights and needs of the child being created. When a person brings a child into the world, regardless of how, they owe that child a duty of care. This duty of care must place the child's needs before the parent's and should include telling the child about their unique origins and genetic parentage. People should process the impacts of their infertility before they become a parent.

It should not be difficult for parents who've spent so much time and effort to create a child using the genetic material of at least one of the parents to understand why genetic connection is also important to the child. They've dedicated time, mental and physical health, and money to ensure a genetic connection—why would a child not feel the same way.

Advancements continued with the introduction of cryopreservation, allowing sperm, eggs, and embryos to be frozen and stored for future use. This was developed in response to the AIDS epidemic. Despite these

advancements, the ART industry remains basically unregulated in the U.S., leading to ethical problems as this is a business whose goal is profit. Instances of mix-ups with sperm, eggs, and embryo specimens have occurred, and alarmingly, there have been cases where doctors have used their own sperm without the knowledge or consent of patients.

As ARTs have become more common, a new generation of donor-conceived individuals is voicing a desire to know their genetic origins. This quest reflects a deep-seated need to understand one's identity and heritage, highlighting the importance of ethical considerations and transparency in the field of assisted reproduction. As the field continues to advance, it's imperative to address the regulatory gaps and respect the rights and desires of all individuals involved, focusing on best interest of the humans we are creating.

Terms Associated with Assisted Reproduction
- **AI** – **Artificial Insemination**: When sperm is directly inserted into a woman's cervix.
- **AID** – **Artificial Insemination by Donor**: When sperm from a donor is inserted into the cervix of a woman in the hopes of creating a pregnancy.
- **ART** - **Assisted Reproductive Technologies**: Fertility treatments where eggs or embryos are handled for the purpose of establishing a pregnancy.
- **Donor Conception:** The process of having a baby using donated sperm, eggs, or embryos. It can involve self-insemination or fertility treatments and sometimes surrogacy.
- **Double Donation:** When both an egg and sperm donor is used to create an embryo who is transplanted into another woman's uterus.
- **Embryo**: An egg fertilized by sperm in the very beginning phase of becoming a fetus.
- **Gametes**: Refers to eggs and sperm, and sometimes people lump embryos in too.
- **Gamete Provider / Donor:** Refers to someone who sells or gives their sperm or eggs to someone or a clinic. People often use 'sperm donor' or 'egg donor' but most do not 'donate' their gametes, they

are paid for them.

- **Gestational Carrier:** This involves the use of IVF where the surrogate does not use her own eggs, and therefore is not genetically related to the baby. This arrangement often provides clearer legal parentage, yet it can also introduce additional medical complexities for the surrogate.
- **GIFT - Gamete Intrafallopian Transfer:** Where an egg is removed and put into the fallopian tube with sperm.
- **ICSI - Intracytoplasmic Sperm Injection:** A single sperm is injected directly into an egg. The fertilized egg (now an embryo) is allowed to develop for a short period in a laboratory setting before it is placed in the uterus.
- **Intended Parent(s):** The parents who use egg and/or sperm provision to become parents (also **Recipient Parent**).
- **IUI – Intrauterine Insemination:** Sperm is placed directly into the uterus.
- **IVF – In Vitro Fertilization:** When an embryo is created outside the body and then placed in a woman's uterus.
- **Recipient Parent:** Is the legal parent of a child conceived through donor conception (also Intended Parent).
- **Solo/Single Mother by Choice (SMBC):** A single woman who chooses to become a mother who does not have a partner. There is also SDBC - solo dad by choice.
- **Surrogacy:** A woman who carries and gives birth to a baby for another couple. Traditional Surrogate means the woman carrying the child uses her egg (also **Gestational Carrier**).
- **Tandem Cycle:** Fertility procedure for creating embryos from donor as well as from either of the intended parents. Results in recipient not knowing which gametes will provide viable embryos—banned in UK & Europe for ethical reasons.
- **ZIFT - Zygote Intrafallopian Transfer:** Where eggs are removed and fertilized, then placed in the woman's fallopian tubes rather than the uterus.

𝒜
attachment

...is the deep emotional bond that forms between individuals, influencing their relationships and emotional responses throughout life.

In a twist reminiscent of "Mommy", "Anchor" explores attachment amid love and turmoil. The characters face fierce devotion and behavioral challenges, mirroring Diane and Steve's intense mother-son bond. Attachment emerges as a lifeline, underscoring the importance of nurturing connections in adversity. The narrative showcases moments of raw emotion and reconciliation, highlighting the resilience and depth of the human spirit. It's a testament to the enduring power of attachment, where love guides through life's tempests, leading to understanding and acceptance and the ability to form secure attachments as an adult.

Anchor (Mommy)

Attachment theory is particularly relevant for individuals who have experienced DNA surprises, were adopted, donor-conceived, or someone with an NPE, leading to separation from one or both genetic parents. It was first proposed by British psychologist John Bowlby in the late 1950s and further developed by Mary Ainsworth in the 1960s and 1970s. This theory sheds light on how the foundational relationships with caregivers, whether genetic or not, deeply influence an individual's emotional landscape and interpersonal dynamics.

For those who grow up separated from their genetic parent(s), understanding the nuances of attachment styles can offer insights into their relational patterns and emotional responses. Secure attachment, characterized by a strong sense of trust and safety in relationships, may be crucial for individuals in these situations, helping them form resilient bonds with raising parent(s) and navigate the complexities of their origins with confidence.

Anxious-ambivalent attachment may manifest in heightened sensitivity to relationships' dynamics, possibly stemming from early uncertainties or inconsistencies in caregiving. This attachment style highlights the need for stability and reassurance in relationships, which can be particularly poignant for those grappling with questions about their identity and belonging.

Avoidant attachment might arise from a subconscious coping mechanism to perceived rejection or neglect, potentially reflecting the complex emotions surrounding the separation from genetic parent(s). This style underscores the challenges in seeking intimacy and support, emphasizing the importance of acknowledging and addressing these barriers to form closer connections.

Disorganized attachment is more prevalent when there's significant disruption in early relationships, including the emotional turmoil of discovering of one's adoption or donor conception under distressing circumstances. This points to the necessity of understanding and healing from these early experiences to foster more stable and secure relationships.

For individuals navigating the emotional terrain of non-traditional family relationships, attachment theory provides a valuable framework to understand how early attachment experiences influence their approach to relationships and self-perception, guiding them toward healing and building more secure, meaningful connections.

B

baby scoop era (BSE)

...is the time period after World War II to the early 1970s, when there was an increased rate of premarital pregnancies and imposed newborn adoption.

In"East of Adoption: The Baby Scoop Times," this era was less about picturesque valleys and more about the turbulent societal currents that led to babies being taken from their mothers. Like the complex family dynamics in Steinbeck's tale, this period was marked by hidden truths, stigma, and silent struggles. It was a time when societal pressures and norms dictated the fates of many, leading to a legacy of lost connections and yearning akin to a Steinbeckian drama. This is a movie where you have no choice, the pressure of society and family force you into an impossible space.

East of Adoption: The Baby Scoop Times
(East of Eden)

This period of time is marked by its profound impact on birth mothers, fathers, and children. An alarming number of newborns were separated from their genetic parents, primarily unwed mothers, due to societal pressures and the stigma associated with out-of-wedlock pregnancies.

For birth mothers, this was a time of immense pain and trauma. Many of these women, often young and vulnerable, were coerced into relinquishing their babies. The prevailing social norms of the time, heavily influenced by moral and religious conservatism, deemed unmarried mothers unfit to raise their children. As a result, countless women were forced into maternity homes where they faced isolation and, in many cases, harsh treatment. The birth of their children was frequently shrouded in secrecy, shame, and stigma leaving lasting psychological scars.

Many birth fathers were either unaware of their children's existence or powerless in the face of societal and familial pressures that favored adoption. Some, due to the prevailing views at the time, blamed the woman for getting pregnant. The father's rights and desires were often ignored, and they were left to deal with the emotional aftermath of lost parenthood in a culture that provided no support for their grief as well.

For the children, the impact was profound and far-reaching. Many adoptees grew up with a sense of loss and identity confusion, compounded by closed adoption practices that sealed their original birth records. This lack of access to their genetic heritage left deep emotional voids, affecting their sense of self and belonging. As these children grew into adults, many began to seek out their genetic roots, often encountering significant challenges and roadblocks. Many of which still exist today. Laws vary state-by-state.

The BSE underscores the damaging effects of societal attitudes and policies that prioritize conformity over the fundamental rights and bonds of genetic families. The era serves as a stark reminder of the need for compassionate, informed approaches to unplanned pregnancies and adoption, emphasizing respect for the wishes and well-being of all parties involved, especially the vulnerable birth mothers and their children. We must acknowledge and learn from this painful part of history.

B

best interest of the child

...is when parent(s) prioritize their child's emotional, psychological, and physical growth to ensure they become well-adjusted adults.

"Little Miss Sunshine: The Road to Adulthood," is a story of a child's journey to becoming a well-adjusted adult, under the watchful eyes of a diverse, loving family. Each family member, with their quirks and wisdom, contributes uniquely to the child's emotional, psychological, and physical growth. Like the film's road trip, life's journey is filled with challenges and triumphs, laughter and learning. This narrative celebrates the ups and downs of growing up, emphasizing the importance of family support in overcoming obstacles and nurturing well-being. It's a reminder that your road to adulthood, though bumpy, can be brightened by familial love and guidance.

Little Miss Sunshine: A Road to Adulthood
(Little Miss Sunshine)

The idea that parents should act in the "best interest of their child" is a fundamental principle that takes on additional layers of complexity in the contexts of assisted reproduction, adoption, and NPEs. When a child is not genetically related to one or both parents due to circumstances such as infertility treatments, donor conception, adoption, or the revelations of an affair or assault, the imperative to prioritize the child's well-being becomes intertwined with the need for transparency and honesty about the child's origins.

Parents must navigate their own complex emotions and traumas related to infertility, the circumstances leading to adoption, or the reasons behind their child's NPE. Prioritizing the child's needs means navigating these personal challenges to ensure the child's narrative is honored and shared with care and respect. This approach not only benefits the child's development but also strengthens the parent-child relationship through a culture of openness and resilience.

The emotional, psychological, and physical development of a child is best supported in an environment where honesty, openness, and the child's right to their own story are upheld from the outset. Telling a child about their unique origins from birth fosters a secure attachment by building a foundation of trust. It eliminates the potential shock or sense of betrayal that can arise from discovering such fundamental truths later in life, which can disrupt the child's sense of identity and belonging and harm the adult child-parent relationship.

Knowing your origins aids in identity formation, allowing them to integrate the various aspects of their heritage and personal history into a cohesive self-image. It also addresses the potential for genetic mirroring concerns, where children might feel disconnected from their family due to perceived or real differences in physical, emotional, or behavioral traits.

Acting in the best interest of the child within the context of non-traditional genetic relationships entails a commitment to honesty, open communication about the child's origins, and a sensitive approach to sharing their unique story. This nurtures a secure attachment, facilitates healthy identity development, and fosters a deep, trusting bond between parent and child, laying the groundwork for the child to grow into a well-adjusted, healthy adult.

B
biological

...is anything pertaining to the science of life or living organisms and their processes.

A cutting-edge theme park boasts genetically revived creatures in modern habitats designed to inhibit their feral tendencies. The twist? The creatures raised in these new environments aren't showing the expected changes, confounding the scientists. The plot thickens as the park's secret is revealed: scientists have been engineering the creatures' DNA to amplify their epigenetic adaptability, attempting to accelerate their evolutionary response to the environment. Chaos erupts when the animals escape their curated environment, exhibiting unforeseen behaviors. The climax reveals these creatures adjusting to both their engineered predispositions and the untamed world, highlighting the complex dance between inherited genes and life's experiences.

Jurassic Genes: The Legacy Unleashed
(Jurassic Park)

Advancements in assisted reproduction are pushing us to redefine our understanding of biological and genetic requiring a more precise use of the terms. We are on the precipice of making a human egg from skin cells, regardless of the gender of the person. This means we are increasingly having to make the distinction between the genetic material that makes us and the environment we grow in.

Biology spans various disciplines, including ecology, anatomy, biochemistry, and physiology, and considers both the genetic blueprint and environmental influences shaping life. Genetics, a specialized branch within biology, focuses on the inheritance and variation of genes, exploring how specific traits and characteristics are transmitted across generations. It can also tell us who our relatives are.

Within this complex landscape, epigenetics acts as bridge, linking genetics with the broader biological interactions influenced by the environment. Epigenetic mechanisms can modify gene activity in response to environmental stimuli, without altering the DNA sequence itself. This means that lifestyle choices and external conditions can impact an individual's health and behavior as well as influence the genetic expression of future generations.

In cases where a child is conceived using a donor egg, the gestational mother's internal environment can induce epigenetic changes in the developing fetus. This underscore the intricate relationship between genetics and biology, where the latter encompasses not only the genetic instructions but also the environmental context in which these instructions are expressed. In such cases, doctors may refer to the mother as the 'biological mother,' acknowledging the potential epigenetic influences she imparts. This challenges the traditional definition of 'biological' mother separating the lines of genetic and environmental impact.

As the boundaries of what defines family and parenthood expand, so too must our language and ethical considerations evolve, reflecting the new realities shaped by these groundbreaking technologies. In the future, we will likely see babies created from genes from multiple people who are raised by non-genetically related parents. The expanding possibilities in reproductive technology not only redefine familial bonds but also how we talk about them.

B

birth certificate (BC)
original birth certificate (OBC)

...is a vital legal record that documents the birth of a person.

Think of your family tree research as starring in "Catch Me If You Can: The Genealogy Edition". Just like Frank Abagnale Jr., birth certificates can be masters of disguise – sometimes the names and details are as forged or untrue as one of Frank's checks. Researching your ancestry here is like being both the detective and the con artist, unraveling truths and fictions, where each document could lead to either a breakthrough, a clever ruse, or a brick wall. Should legal documents have half-truths? It's a heartbreaking chase through history, with the accuracy of your family story always seeming one step ahead, like Leo DiCaprio in a pilot's uniform.

Catch Me If You Can: Genealogy Edition
(Catch Me If You Can)

This official document typically includes the name of the Individual given at birth, the exact time and date when the individual was born, the specific location where the birth occurred, the names of the legal parents, and possibly the hospital or location of birth, the attending physician or midwife, and the birth weight and length of the newborn. How this document is used for legal versus societal purposes is very different.

When someone is adopted a new birth certificate is issued. The name of the child as well as the name of the parents is changed and sometimes the date and place of birth are altered or removed. A new birth certificate is issued to take the place of the OBC. The original document is then sealed and is often only available through a court order which in some states can be very difficult and costly to obtain.

The law sees a BC as a document to show the age of a child and who is legally responsible for that child. So if little Timmy hits a baseball into the neighbor's window, everyone knows who is responsible for the bill. Once a child is 22 (after college age), it doesn't really matter to the law who is responsible for the child because they are now an adult.

For societal purposes though, birth certificates are used as a vital resource in genealogical research for connecting different generations to trace ancestry back through time. If you have a DNA surprise, are adopted, donor-conceived, have an NPE, or are misattributed, your birth certificate doesn't show your genetic parents. Not having accurate records leads to mistaken ancestry, medical issues, and heritage. Many would like to change this legal record to reflect the truth of their origins. This is very difficult in most states and impossible in some.

It is important that every state provide a means to update birth certificates to include both genetic parents and raising parents; this would be a 'long form' birth certificate. A short form with just raising legal parents would be available to show proof of parentage or age of the child. Once a person attains adulthood, they could access their long form certificate with all parental information. This way there will be an accurate record for future generations of all the parents who influenced and shaped who we are and no one will be left wondering about their heritage, medical history, or identity.

B

birth certificate parent
(birth certificate father - BCF / birth certificate mother - BCM)

...is the name of your father or mother on your birth certificate (who may or may not have raised you or be genetically related to you).

Imagine your story as "The Born Identity." Just like Jason Bourne seeking to uncover his true identity, you're on a mission to discover the real story behind your BCF and BCM. It's a thrilling journey filled with plot twists and cryptic clues, where the names on your birth certificate might lead to surprising revelations or unexpected dead ends. As you delve deeper, you realize that figuring out who you really are can be as complex and action-packed as any spy adventure, complete with hidden histories and mysterious connections.

The Born Identity (The Bourne Identity)

23

In most states, when a woman is married at the time she gives birth, her husband is presumed to be the legal father and named on the birth certificate. If the mother wishes to name someone else, a legal proceeding is required. Procedures vary by state but typically involve genetic testing, relinquishment of parental rights by the husband, and acknowledgment by the genetic father. If not married, whomever she lists as father would sign either a Voluntary Acknowledgment of Paternity (VAP) or a Paternity Affidavit. She can also not name a father.

It is important to recognize that the individuals named on the birth certificate are legally responsible for the child. This includes rights and obligations pertaining to custody, child support, and inheritance. With adoption, assisted reproduction, and NPEs, the birth certificate may list non-genetic parents, reflecting the child's legal parentage rather than genetic lineage. Being named a parent to a child on their birth certificate does not necessarily mean a genetic connection for both the mother and the father.

The court's primary consideration in these matters is often the best interests of the child which in the past has included emotional and financial support and stability, with a nod to the right to know their genetic heritage. Our understanding of stability has evolved. We used to believe you could substitute a new care provider for a child and the child would not know the difference. We now know this can severely impact the child's emotional and psychological wellbeing exponentially more than growing up knowing they have different genetic parents.

As medical technology advances we are also discovering the need to know our family medical history is vital to our health. This shift in understanding the mental and medical health consequences underscores the need for legal reforms that accommodate the complexities of modern families and reproductive technologies, particularly as it pertains to the child's right to understand their genetic origins.

Our current system, however, does not allow for both the legal and genetic parents to be named on the birth certificate. This limitation highlights the need for updated birth certificate laws that acknowledge and reflect the diverse structures of modern families while protecting the rights and best interests of the child and future generations.

B

black market baby

...is a child who is illegally sold and adopted (not through the mainstream legal adoption market).

Imagine a plot twist in the style of "The Italian Job". Instead of a slick heist of gold bars through the streets of Venice, the treasure is far more precious. A covert team not of thieves but shadowy figures in the murky waters of illegal baby trade traffics babies. Each plays a critical role, from the smooth-talker who convinces a desperate parent, to the attorney who crafts fake documents. As they dodge the law and moral quandaries, they orchestrate a heist where the 'gold' is a baby, and the 'getaway car' is a stroller. The twists and turns of this operation reveal the intricate and often heartbreaking realities of black market adoptions, where every decision has a lifelong impact on the child at the heart of their plot.

The Crib Job: A Black Market Baby's Tale
(The Italian Job)

In the underworld of adoption, a black market baby involves a financial transaction where payment is made to either the genetic parents, an adoption attorney, an adoption facilitator, an agency, or another intermediary in order to bypass legal adoption processes. Those involved in the adoption of a black market baby may face criminal prosecution, and the child could potentially be removed from the adoptive raising parents and placed with new ones or returned to the genetic parents.

Historically, especially in the early 1900s, a lack of regulation and shifting social attitudes created an environment conducive to black market adoptions. Notorious groups such as Cole babies, Hicks babies, Bessie babies, Dr. Mary babies, Butterbox babies, and Springer babies emerged during this era. Or more recently from the 1970s to the mid-2000s where hospital staff were implicated in trafficking babies in the country of Georgia.

Often, these children were born to impoverished or single mothers who were either deceived or pressured into relinquishing their babies. In some cases, mothers were falsely informed that their babies had died, when in reality, they were trafficked to adoptive families, with the facilitator making a huge fee.

The repercussions of black market adoption extend beyond legal consequences. The emotional toll on all parties is profound. The child may experience lasting emotional trauma from being separated from their genetic family combined with the traumatic circumstances of the removal from their family. For the genetic family, the pain of loss can be overwhelming. Especially if they were not involved in the adoption and were either tricked into relinquishing their child or lied to. Similarly, adoptive families, entangled in a web of lies and hidden truths, often live under the shadow of these deceptions. The practice of concealing such significant information can lead to a festering of secrets, deeply affecting the family dynamics and individual psychological well-being of the raising adoptive parents and the child.

C

centimorgan (cM)

...is a unit of measure in DNA shared between two people used to estimate familial relationships.

Think "National Treasure", but the quest is for your family roots, not gold. A band of genealogy enthusiasts embark on an epic journey, using centimorgans and other DNA clues as their guide. Each shared DNA segment leads to new untold stories and relatives, like a treasure map of heritage. They decode genetic clues and unearth ancestral secrets, realizing the real treasure is the family connections and lost stories they find for you along the way. This adventure isn't just about finding where you come from, but also discovering the rich tapestry of relationships and family history that centimorgans can reveal, and helping people to know and understand their genetic identity and family story.

Genetic Treasure: The Centimorgan Map
(National Treasure)

27

Direct-to-consumer (DTC) DNA tests like AncestryDNA, Family Tree DNA, MyHeritage, and 23andMe, have become a popular tool for exploring genetic heritage and discovering familial connections. Central to these discoveries is the concept of DNA matches, which occur when two individuals share a significant amount of DNA, indicating a familial relationship. The shared DNA is measured in centimorgans (cM), a unit that helps estimate how related two individuals might be.

DTC DNA tests analyze an individual's genome and compare it to others in their database. When significant similarities are found, these are reported as DNA matches. The amount of shared DNA is crucial in determining the potential relationship. For example, half siblings typically share between 1,160 to 2,436 cM, while first cousins usually share between 396 to 1,397 cM. This is why it can be difficult to know if someone is a half sibling or a first cousin. The exact number varies due to the random nature of DNA inheritance. While Ancestry, Family Tree DNA, and MyHeritage display the shared DNA in centimorgans, 23andMe presents it as a percentage of shared DNA.

Interpreting these numbers and understanding the specific family connections they indicate can be challenging. This is where tools like DNA Painter come into play. DNA Painter is an online resource that allows individuals to input the number of centimorgans or the percentage of DNA shared with a match. It then provides a range of possible relationships based on this data, using known statistical probabilities to suggest whether a match is likely a first cousin, half-sibling, grandparent, or some other relative. Check out 'What Are The Odds' (WATO) too.

This feature is particularly valuable for adoptees, donor-conceived individuals, and those with non-paternal events (NPEs). For these groups, DTC DNA tests can be a gateway to uncovering genetic family connections that might have been previously unknown or unconfirmed. By understanding the centimorgans shared with matches and using tools like DNA Painter, they can begin to piece together their genetic heritage and connect with relatives.

Total centimorgans shared empower individual to explore their genetic roots, establish connections with genetic family members, and gain valuable insights into their ancestry and personal history.

C

cognitive dissonance

... is the mental conflict some parents face between the reality of their child's genetic origins and the desire for their child to be genetically theirs, leading to the subconscious suppression of the truth.

"Echoes of Reality" is a tale of parents caught in a tangle of truth and wishes in the psychological maze of cognitive dissonance. As they navigate a world where their beliefs about their child's genetic origins clash with reality, their minds warp time and memory like the time-travel paradox in "Predestination". Each revelation, like a twist in time, unravels and reweaves their understanding, challenging their perception of truth and identity. Reality becomes a perception shaped by deep-seated desires and fears, echoing the complex dance of cognitive dissonance.

Echoes of Reality (Predestination)

Cognitive dissonance (CD), a concept introduced by psychologist Leon Festinger, is particularly relevant in the context of parents raising children who are not genetically related to them. This psychological phenomenon occurs when the parent experiences a conflict between the truth and their actions, desires, and beliefs. In loss of genetic continuity context, this means hiding a child's genetic origins while maintaining a narrative of honesty and openness within the family and wishing their child was genetically related to them. This internal conflict can lead to significant psychological discomfort.

Parents might find themselves in a complex emotional predicament, where the act of withholding crucial genetic information from their child contradicts their moral values or understanding of parental responsibility. This dissonance can arise from various sources, such as social stigma, personal guilt, or fear of disrupting family dynamics.

The struggle to maintain a consistent self-image while managing this hidden truth can lead to various coping mechanisms. Some parents might rationalize their decision to keep the secret, perhaps by emphasizing their role in the child's upbringing over genetic ties. Others might suppress or deny the importance of genetic information to reduce their discomfort.

Cognitive dissonance in these scenarios may not just be an individual issue but can be influenced by broader societal and cultural factors. Societal norms and expectations about family, parenthood, and lineage can significantly impact parents' decisions to disclose or conceal such information. The fear of social judgment, shame, or the potential upheaval of revealing the truth can intensify the psychological conflict.

In some cases, some parents over time may push the truth so far into their subconscious, they no longer remember it. This phenomenon is shown in extreme medical cases where the life of their child depends on accurate genetic medical information and the parent insists they are the genetic parent and their medical history is applicable. Ultimately, cognitive dissonance in the context of raising parents who have concealed genetic information of their children highlights the complex interplay between personal beliefs and desires, societal norms, and ethical considerations.

C

coming out

...is the act of publicly acknowledging and embracing the truth about one's genetic origins.

In "Erased Origins" Jamie discovers he is donor-conceived. In a conservative community where lineage defines identity, Jamie's revelation threatens to unravel tightly held family secrets. Like the emotional journey in "Boy Erased", Jamie navigates the complexities of coming out about his genetic past, confronting familial pressures and societal expectations. This film weaves a tale of truth-seeking and self-acceptance, challenging the notion of what truly makes a family. As Jamie steps into the light of his reality, he faces a crossroads: to embrace this newfound identity or protect the family facade. This is a story of courage, the search for authenticity, and the power of owning one's story in the face of adversity.

Erased Origins (Boy Erased)

Coming out in the context of discovering and revealing a hidden genetic identity from adoption, donor conception, or an NPE is a deeply personal journey that involves publicly acknowledging a fundamental truth about one's genetic origins. This process can be as emotionally complex and challenging as coming out about one's sexual orientation, as it involves not just self-acceptance but also the risk of altering existing relationships and facing potential judgment or misunderstanding from your raising family, friends, new genetic family, and society.

For individuals in these situations, coming out often signifies a significant shift in identity. Discovering that one or both of their parents are not genetically related to you can trigger a cascade of emotions: shock, confusion, anger, a sense of betrayal, and a need to redefine their understanding of family and self. This revelation can shatter long-held beliefs and narratives about their background, heritage, and raising family.

The act of coming out in these contexts is not just about sharing a fact; it's about seeking validation and understanding for a newly discovered aspect of one's identity. It can be a daunting experience, fraught with fear of rejection or judgment. Family members may react with denial, anger, or hurt, not just because of the news itself but also because of the implications it carries about family secrets and truths. Friends and extended family might struggle to understand or accept this new reality, leading to a sense of isolation for the individual.

Moreover, coming out can be a journey of navigating legal and ethical complexities. Questions about the right to know one's genetic origins, the implications for familial relationships, and the handling of such sensitive information adds layers of complexity to the process. Amidst these challenges, coming out can also be a path to empowerment and authenticity. It allows individuals to embrace their full story, understand their roots more deeply, and form more honest relationships. It can lead to joining supportive communities of others with similar experiences, providing a sense of belonging and understanding.

C

constellation

...is an inclusive framework that encompasses all individuals impacted by genetic continuity loss.

This film focuses on a constellation of lives influenced by the loss of genetic continuity. In each era, characters face challenges related to identity, heritage, and genetic lineage. In the 1800s a person learns of their father's infertility and genetic family; a genealogist in the 20th century uncovers a hidden family line; a futuristic individual has six genetic parents from advanced genetic technologies. As their stories unfold, echoing themes of connection, family, and belonging, emerge. These narratives, separated by time and space, reveal the profound impact of genetic ties on everyone, the human yearning to understand one's place in the continuum of life, and how interconnected families and generations are.

Constellation: Echoes Through Time (Cloud Atlas)

33

The term Adoption Constellation was initially introduced by psychologist Michael Grand. he term Constellation is used to represent the three groups in adoption: the child, raising (adoptive) parents, and the genetic (birth) parents. The concept is vitally important when discussing genetic continuity loss because it encompasses the wide-reaching ripple effects that extend horizontally across various individuals and vertically into the unique experiences of each person within this community.

Horizontally, the term 'Constellation' acknowledges that genetic continuity loss touches the lives of a multitude of individuals. This includes anyone whose life is impacted by genetic continuity loss as a member of this complex network. This includes not only genetic parents, raising parents, and the adult-child (DCP/adoptees/person with an NPE, their significant other and children, as well as siblings, the extended family (both genetic and raising), and friends.

Recognizing this broad impact is crucial because it highlights the interconnectedness of all these individuals. It acknowledges that the effects of genetic continuity loss radiate through family structures, affecting not just the immediate participants but also a wide circle of relatives and loved ones. Understanding the constellation allows for a more comprehensive appreciation of how this issue reverberates across families and society and how diverse relationships are influenced.

Vertically, within the Constellation, each individual's experience is unique and deeply personal. It accounts for how every person navigates the complexities of genetic continuity loss, from genetic parents grappling with the decision to relinquish a child or donate gametes to adoptees/DCP/NPE seeking their genetic roots and to understand their identity, medical history, and place in the world and their expanded family, to raising parents trying to have confidence in their role.

By acknowledging both the horizontal and vertical impacts, the concept of the Constellation emphasizes the breadth and depth of this issue. It recognizes the collective experiences of an entire community while respecting the individual journeys of each member. This holistic perspective fosters empathy, understanding, and support among those who are part of the genetic continuity loss constellation.

C

cross sibling

...is your genetic half sibling's other genetic half sibling that you are not genetically related to.

Here we confront an intricate network of half-siblings, cross-siblings, siblings, and family ties that rival the most complex of spider webs. Peter Parker must navigate this maze of relationships, swinging from one family branch to another, discovering connections he never knew he had. His dad Richard had a son named Matt with his first wife, and Matt has a half sister Sue from his mom and her new husband. Peter and Sue are the "cross siblings" at the center of this tale. As the family gathers for a reunion, they untangle the web of who's who, learning that genetics may be one definition of siblings, but it's love and camaraderie that binds all siblings together in this heartwarming comedy of errors and affections.

FAMILY TIES

The Family Web (Spider-Man: Into the Spider-Verse)

Cross siblings, a term emerging from the complex narratives of modern families, refers to those individuals who share a half-sibling but are not genetically related to each other. This kinship arises in the lives of those who are donor-conceived, adopted, have experienced a non-paternal event (NPE), or are part of blended families with stepparents. Cross siblings occupy a unique space in the familial landscape, where blood ties intersect with the bonds formed through family and shared experiences and traditions.

While genetics play a significant role in our draw towards individuals who share our traits, the definition of family extends beyond the confines of DNA. The relationships with those we grow alongside, those we share our triumphs and challenges with, are just as profound. Family should be conceptualized as inclusive, not exclusive, recognizing that our capacity to love and connect is not finite.

Cross siblings exemplify the idea that family is a tapestry of connections—some threads are woven by shared genes, while others are colored by shared lives. These connections are not a matter of 'either-or' but 'both-and.' In the broader view of kinship, a cross sibling can be as significant in one's life as any genetic relative. The shared history, the inside jokes, the mutual support during difficult times—all these elements contribute to the richness of the relationship. Or you can build such relationships with newly discovered cross siblings.

Embracing cross siblings is about recognizing the value in all forms of family, acknowledging that the families we make can be as integral to our identity as the families we're born into. It's about seeing family not just as a genetic fact but as a social construct, one that is ever evolving and expansive.

We find celebration in the diverse ways in which families come together. It's an acknowledgment that love is not limited by genetic similarity but also by choice, an act of inclusion. By embracing cross siblings, we open our hearts to a more nuanced understanding of family, one that honors all the various ways people can be tied to one another. It's a vision of family that is generous, compassionate, and boundless, reflecting the myriad ways in which humans connect, care, and commit to one another in the journey of life.

D

dibbling
(some DCP don't favor this term)

...is what some donor-conceived people call their half-siblings via donor conception.

In this plot twist we focus on a group of dibblings navigating the complexities and joys of being part of a large, unconventional family created through assisted reproduction. The film humorously and heartwarmingly explores their journey of discovering and connecting with each other and managing the dynamics of a rapidly expanding family tree. It's a celebration of the unique bonds shared by dibblings, highlighting the laughter, challenges, shared synchronicities, and love that come with being part of such a diverse and extensive family network. It is dibblings who truly understand the challenges of being donor conceived.

Ten Dozen: The Dibbling Edition (Cheaper by Dozen)

Navigating the world of donor-conceived people (DCP) and their siblings, often referred to as 'dibblings', presents unique challenges and emotional complexities. For DCP, the journey starts with the fundamental knowledge of their conception – some grow up aware of their status, while others experience a DNA surprise, transforming them into a late discovery donor-conceived person (LDDCP).

There's an innate pull towards genetic relatives, a yearning to connect with those who share genetic ties. This connection is not just about curiosity; it's about genetic mirroring—seeing oneself reflected in others, recognizing shared traits, likes and dislikes, and tendencies that forge a deeper understanding of self. Fellow dibblings understand the DCP journey: the commodification of origins, intentional separation of family, expected existential gratitude for your birth, parental shame, and cultural stereotyping. But what happens when this quest for connection uncovers not just a few, but potentially hundreds of half-siblings?

Managing large half-sibling groups (or pods as some say) requires more than just an emotional investment; it calls for strategic approaches. Imagine the daunting task of keeping track of numerous siblings and their extended families, each with unique stories, backgrounds, and milestones. Organizing inclusive gatherings becomes a logistical puzzle, where every piece matters, and every individual seeks a sense of belonging.

For those new to the sibling group, the integration process can be overwhelming. It's not just about adding another name to the list; it's about welcoming a new life, a new set of experiences into an already intricate family tapestry. The emotional landscape of these relationships is vast – from the joy of new connections to the anxiety of fitting into an established group, and the inevitable questions about what 'family' truly means.

DCP and their dibblings must navigate this complex web of relationships, exploring ways to foster meaningful connections while maintaining their individuality. They must find a balance between the excitement of expanding their family circle and the emotional toll it can take. These relationships challenge traditional notions of family, pushing the boundaries of what it means to belong and be connected.

𝒟

direct-to-consumer (DTC) DNA test

...is an over-the-counter genetic analysis service used to uncover ancestry information, health predispositions, and genetic relationships.

In "Gattaca: the DNA Discovery", the focus shifts to the personal and often surprising journey of DTC DNA test results. Similar to the original film's exploration of genetic determinism, this adaptation delves into the revelations and ethical dilemmas faced by people as they uncover hidden aspects of their ancestry and health predispositions. While each story is unique, they share a surprising number of similarities. This film juxtaposes the themes of destiny and choice, mirroring the "Gattaca" narrative, but within the context of modern genetic testing and its impact on personal identity, family secrets, family, and societal perceptions.

Gattaca: The DNA Discovery (Gattaca)

Direct-to-consumer (DTC) DNA tests have transformed the landscape of genetic exploration, offering individuals unprecedented access to information about their ancestry, health, and genetic connections. This revolution in genetic testing began to take shape in the early 2000s, following the completion of the Human Genome Project in 2003, which significantly advanced our understanding of genetics. We've learned this was just the beginning in this nascent science.

The most common types of DTC DNA tests is autosomal DNA testing, primarily used for ancestry purposes. These tests provide a wealth of insights, including ethnicity estimates and the identification of genetic relatives across both maternal and paternal lines. The first test was sold by 23 and Me in 2007. With over 30 million people in the U.S. having taken a DTC test as of 2020, it has become increasingly easy to discover genetic family ties - if you haven't tested, your third cousin probably has.

The leading companies in this field include:

- **23andMe:** includes health reports, genetic risk factors, and DNA relative matching; the 2nd largest database.
- **AncestryDNA:** Known for its genealogy testing kits, they have the largest database of all companies.
- **Family Tree DNA:** pioneered DTC DNA testing for genealogy purposes, their tests now include Y-DNA and mitochondrial DNA testing, as well as autosomal DNA.
- **MyHeritage:** focuses on international genealogy and caters to a global audience.

DTC DNA testing has gained immense popularity as people are drawn to the personal connection, sense of identity, and the opportunity to explore their ancestors' lives and legacies. These tests enable people to uncover their ancestral origins, connect with their heritage, and make informed decisions about their health. People triangulate their matches to identify genetic relatives. Websites like DNA Painter and What Are The Odds (WATO) are useful tools to assist with this process.

DTC DNA tests also come with privacy and misuse concerns. Some fear unauthorized access to their data, sharing with third parties without consent, or potential discrimination based on their genetic information. Historical traumas have led some communities to be cautious about engaging in DTC DNA testing. But in the U.S., the cat is out of the bag.

D

disenfranchised grief

...is the emotional pain experienced when a loss is not openly acknowledged, socially validated, or publicly mourned.

This film depicts the silent turmoil of disenfranchised grief. The protagonist has a DNA surprise and learns her genetic father is deceased and struggles with what feels like erased memories in the original film. She morns the loss of someone she's never met and the memories she'll never make. This is an exploration of unvalidated sorrow, underscoring the necessity for societal acknowledgment and the therapeutic power of giving a voice to suppressed emotions. The protagonist's journey of self-discovery reveals the profound impact of ambiguous loss and the resilience required to seek validation in a world that often overlooks such pain.

Eternal Hidden Grief (Eternal Sunshine of the Spotless Mind)

Disenfranchised grief, a term first coined by Dr. Kenneth Doka, a professor of Gerontology, is a form of mourning that lacks societal recognition and validation. It is a poignant reality for DCP, adoptees, and individuals with an NPE. This grief is complex, as it encompasses not just the mourning of a person or a relationship but also the loss of a self-identity, a perceived family history, and the anticipated future connections that might never be.

The journey of reunion for adoptees, DCP, and people with an NPE often leads to the discovery of deceased close genetic relatives. They find themselves grieving for someone they never met and mourning the lost opportunity for connection and the answers that died with their relative. This grief is twofold: it's the pain of losing a relative and the sorrow for what could have been: conversations, shared moments, hugs, and an understanding of origins.

People with a DNA surprise face a profound upheaval of their identity. The revelation that a parent they grew up with is not their genetic parent shatters their understanding of their family narrative. They grieve for their past self, the family they thought they knew, and their relationship(s) with the parent(s) who raised them. This experience reshapes their sense of belonging and the foundation upon which they've built their life and sense of self.

This disenfranchised grief is further compounded by the lack of societal acknowledgment. These forms of loss are not typically recognized in public discourses or rituals, leaving individuals to navigate their grief in isolation. They must grapple with complex emotions without the usual societal support systems that accompany recognized forms of mourning and loss.

The journey of discovering and connecting with genetic relatives can be bittersweet. The joy of finding new family members is often tempered by the reality of the relationships and time lost even when they are not deceased. Disenfranchised grief becomes a silent companion on the journey towards self-discovery. This underscores the importance of enhancing societal understanding and support systems to acknowledge all types of grief, particularly those experienced outside traditional contexts, such as by DCP, adoptees, individuals with an NPE, and those with a DNA surprise.

𝒟

DNA search angel

...is someone who assists people in identifying their genetic parent(s) without compensation.

A dedicated DNA Search Angel embarks on a journey to unravel the tangled web of ancestry and identity in "Family Forward". Instead of random acts of kindness, they perform acts of genetic detective work, tirelessly aiding people in discovering their genetic origins and navigating the labyrinth of ancestry databases and family trees. Each person who finds their genetic truth tells their family and friends, creating a ripple effect of discovery and new beginnings. DNA Angels don't just connect genetic dots, they weave a tapestry of familial connections. We witness the power of knowing one's roots, reminding us that sometimes, the most significant inheritance lies within our genes and we just need a little help to find it.

Family Forward (Pay It Forward)

43

DNA Search Angels are genealogists by passion or profession who dedicate their time and expertise to solving genetic identity mysteries. These Angels, some with formal training in genealogy and others armed with extensive hands-on experience, assist people in uncovering the identities of their genetic parents. Their work is a blend of science, history, and detective work, driven by a commitment to bring clarity and insights to those seeking to understand their genetic origins.

Utilizing a variety of tools and methods, they often begin with DTC DNA tests, which have become increasingly popular and accessible. These tests provide crucial genetic links that can be the starting point in unraveling a person's genetic history. The Angels meticulously build family trees, tracing up and down your list of DNA matches. This process involves studying each match's genetic relationship to the person in question, often delving into several generations to find a connection.

They also use a plethora of resources including social media, obituaries, newspaper archives, and census books. Obituaries and newspapers often contain family histories and connections that are not immediately evident in genetic data. Census records offer insights into family compositions and locations at specific points in time, helping to build a more complete picture of a person's ancestry.

Once potential family connections are established, DNA Search Angels employ a method known as triangulation. This technique involves comparing the DNA of three or more individuals to determine if they share a common ancestor. Through this method, Angels can verify the accuracy of their findings, ensuring they have identified the correct individuals.

The work of a DNA Search Angel goes beyond mere genealogical research; it is a deeply personal and often emotional journey. They bring to light family stories, lost connections, and unexpected truths. Their role is pivotal in helping individuals piece together their identities, often filling voids in their personal histories with newfound knowledge and understanding. The dedication and compassion of DNA Search Angels in their quest to connect people with their genetic roots make them unsung heroes in the realm of personal discovery and identity.

🎥 **44** The nonprofit organization *DNAngels* assists people in identifying genetic parents for free.

𝒟

DNA surprise

...is an unexpected revelation about one's ancestry, parentage, or genetic makeup that is often uncovered through a DTC DNA test.

In a twist on the film "Memento", where the main character uses notes and tattoos to piece together his past after suffering from short-term memory loss, this is a story about an individual who reconstructs their ancestry following a DNA surprise. The protagonist, armed with genetic clues and fragmented family stories, must trace the scattered pieces of their heritage to form a complete picture of their identity. This narrative captures the suspense and piecemeal discovery process of "Memento", but within the context of genealogy and personal history, offering a clever and poignant commentary on the journey to self-understanding.

Memento: The Hidden Lineage (Memento)

45

A DNA surprise, usually stemming from a DTC DNA test, can be a deeply traumatic experience, leading to an identity crisis and straining familial relationships. It can profoundly alter an individual's sense of self and family. It is often described by those affected as a moment of time slowing down where everything previously believed to be true is suddenly called into question and you are untethered from your world and sense of self. The impacts span a wide spectrum, ranging from minimal to some experiencing significant trauma and emotional upheaval.

For many, learning they have an NPE, are a Late Discovery Adoptee (LDA), or a Late Discovery Donor-Conceived Person (LDDCP) is vividly etched in memory. The shock of learning about one's true genetic identity uproots your sense of belonging and place in your raising family. Many report a difficulty looking in the mirror as they no longer recognize the person they see because their physical features now seem to belong to some unknown person.

This upheaval extends to the dynamics within a person's raising family. What were believed to be full siblings may now be half-siblings. The revelation may uncover a parent's affair or fertility struggles, leading to feelings of betrayal, confusion, and anger. The parent-adult child relationship is significantly impacted when such fundamental truths are withheld or misrepresented. People feel a sense of betrayal because they were lied to by their raising parent(s), someone we inherently trust.

The ripple effects of a DNA surprise also touches the individual's nuclear family. Spouses or partners often find themselves supporting their loved one through this complex emotional journey, while children grapple with the redefined genetic history of their family and perhaps even their ethnicity.

Upon identifying new genetic family, there's a drive to connect and understand one's origins—to see who you resemble, to learn where your traits originate from, to know your medical history. While the initial response is shock, it is frequently followed by a sense of validation and understanding.

Navigating a DNA surprise involves not only confronting and reassessing one's identity but also redefining relationships and rebuilding trust. It's a journey that reshapes family narratives, challenges deeply held beliefs, and, ultimately, can lead to a more complete understanding of oneself.

D

donor (sperm/egg/embryo)
sometimes the term gamete provider is used

...is someone who sells or gives their sperm, eggs, or embryos to someone or a clinic.

Like "The Delivery Man", "Genetic Consignor" follows a young man's life as a sperm donor who was initially motivated by financial need. As he matures, he confronts the unanticipated consequences of his past decisions: the existence of numerous genetic children seeking their genetic origins. The story blends humor with the poignant journey of self-discovery and responsibility. It explores the donor's growing awareness and emotional responses to the reality of his widespread genetic legacy, shedding light on the profound implications of gamete donation and the deep-seated human desire for connection, identity, and the need for regulation of the fertility industry.

Genetic Consignor (The Delivery Man)

47

Donating sperm, eggs, or embryos, a process more accurately termed gamete provision due to the often involved compensation, carries deep-seated emotional and ethical implications that many donors, especially the young, may not fully comprehend at the time of their contribution. This oversight becomes evident when donor-conceived children, driven by an innate need, seek out their genetic origins. They desire to understand who they resemble, the traits that define them, and crucial aspects of their medical and family history.

For donors, particularly those who donated in their youth without fully grasping the long-term impact of their decision, the emergence of genetic offspring seeking a connection can be an overwhelming experience. The realization that they have played a significant role in the creation of life, contributing to the existence of individuals who share half of their genetic material, can lead to profound introspection.

This revelation challenges the donors' perceptions, confronting them with a sense of responsibility towards these genetic offspring. It raises complex questions about the nature of parenthood, legacy, and the bonds that tie individuals together. Moreover, it can have far-reaching implications on the donors' current familial and social dynamics, particularly if they have established families unaware of their past decisions.

The challenges faced by gamete providers underscore the need for more comprehensive counseling and education about the long-term implications of gamete and embryo provision. It is crucial for potential donors to understand not only the medical procedures and future possible physical impacts involved but also the emotional and ethical dimensions of their decision. This understanding is vital to ensure that donors are making informed decisions they can reconcile in the future, as the effects of their actions extend into the lives of others and across generations.

For some donor-conceived people, the term 'gamete provider' more accurately reflects the transactional nature of the process, moving away from the traditional notion of altruistic 'donation.' This shift in terminology acknowledges the complexities and nuances of gamete provision, respecting the perspectives and experiences of all parties involved in this intricate web of life creation.

𝒟

donor-conceived person (DCP)
donor-conceived individual (DCI)

...is an individual who was conceived through assisted reproductive using donated sperm, eggs, or embryos.

"The DCP Dive" follows a DCP on a mission to uncover the truth about their origins. Like navigating through dreams within dreams like in "Inception", they delve into the depths of their genetic history, unraveling the layers of medical science, donor anonymity, and family dynamics in their raising family and newly discovered genetic family including many siblings. The narrative intertwines reality and revelation, exploring the emotional and existential questions that arise from being donor-conceived. It's an exploration of identity, origin, family, and the profound impact of donor conception on individuals and families.

Inception: The DCP Dive (Inception)

Navigating life as a Donor-Conceived Person/People (DCP) comes with a unique set of challenges and emotional complexities. For those who grow up knowing about their conception, as they become adults there's often a pull to understand their genetic roots and seek out genetic connections. This journey of coming out of the 'FOG' of unawareness can be a profound experience of self-discovery. For Late Discovery Donor-Conceived People (LDDCP), the shock of learning their origins through a DTC DNA test, finding paperwork, or someone who 'spills the beans' can bring a whirlwind of emotions, from disbelief to anger, to a deep sense of betrayal.

Historically, the practice of assisted reproduction was shrouded in secrecy. Doctors advised recipient parents of donor gametes to maintain the illusion of genetic parenthood, even suggesting intimate relations to coincide with procedures to obscure the child's genetic origins. Such practices have led to a generation of individuals with misattributed parentage. Only recently are parents encouraged to embrace their child's donor-conceived identity from an early age and to tell their children their origin story from birth.

The commodification of human gametes adds another layer of complexity, as DCP grapple with the realization that their very existence began as a transaction. The intentional separation from their genetic parent can evoke feelings of loss and a yearning for a missing piece of their identity which can be acute due to a lack of genetic mirroring and no explanation as to why they are 'different' from other family members. There's an expected gratitude towards their raising parents and the life they've been given, which can conflict with the natural curiosity about their genetic origins.

DCP often face social gaslighting, where their desire to know their genetic family is downplayed or dismissed. The lack of genetic mirroring leaves many feeling isolated and different, struggling with genetic bewilderment and an identity crisis. The potential health implications of unknown or incorrect medical history add to the anxiety.

The path to reunion is fraught with emotional stress, shared by both DCP and LDDCP alike. While the search for genetic family can be a blessing, leading to meaningful connections, it can also end in rejection or uncover painful family secrets or distressing medical information. The pervasive secrecy surrounding their conception, particularly for LDDCP, often translates into feelings of betrayal and anger towards raising parents who withheld the truth.

In this complex web of genetic, psychological, and social factors, DCP are forging their path, advocating for transparency and the dismantling of the secrecy that has long governed the world of assisted reproduction. They are redefining what family means, challenging societal norms, and seeking acknowledgment for their unique experiences and the right to their genetic history. As they navigate these waters, DCP are finding solidarity with each other, creating a community where their voices can be heard and their experiences validated.

In the face of these challenges, the necessity for community becomes a lifeline for DCP. Support groups, therapy, and online communities offer solace and understanding. In these spaces, DCP can share their experiences, find comfort in not being alone, and receive guidance on navigating the emotional terrain of their unique circumstances. These support systems not only help with coping and healing but also serve as platforms for advocacy and change, pushing for more ethical practices in assisted reproduction.

A critical issue for DCP is the lack of comprehensive data on the number of individuals conceived through gamete donation worldwide. This absence of tracking and regulation increases the risk of sexual relationships with unknown close genetic relatives, a concern particularly acute in areas with a high concentration of donor-conceived individuals. It underscores the importance of accessible genetic information and transparency in donor conception, to prevent genetic siblings from unknowingly entering into romantic relationships, have accurate medical history of one's life, and to empower DCP with knowledge about their origins.

As the community of DCP continues to grow and connect, there's an emerging collective voice calling for change. This voice advocates for the rights to genetic knowledge, the dismantling of secrecy, and the establishment of ethical guidelines to protect the well-being of those conceived through donor gametes.

In the U.S. there is almost no regulations on assisted reproduction like in Europe and the U.K. U.S. DCPs are advocating to officially end anonymity, for required genetic testing of gametes, limits on the number of families that can use one donor, information and counseling for donors before they donate to understand the risks and responsibilities, education and counseling for recipient parents, and free a mechanism for an ongoing exchange of medical and familial information. Through solidarity and support, DCP are creating a future where the complexities of donor conception are met with openness and understanding, and where their identities are acknowledged and respected in the full light of truth.

_E_
epigenetics

...is how environmental factors and individual behaviors can influence gene expression without altering the DNA sequence itself.

"Echoes of the Tide" is a tale of family and the unseen forces that shape us. The Sullivan family seems ordinary, but there is a legacy of unspoken trauma. The patriarch, a stoic survivor of profound hardship, unknowingly passes more than just his DNA to his children—he transmits echoes of his past sorrows. The plot thickens as his daughter, an aspiring geneticist, uncovers the hidden strands of their family's legacy, revealing how the shadows of one generation can subtly impact the next. Through her eyes, we explore the fascinating and complex world of epigenetics, where our ancestors' experiences resonate in the genetic whispers of today in ways we never imagined.

Echoes of the Tides (The Prince of Tides)

53

Conrad Waddington, a British developmental biologist in the 1940s, introduced the term "epigenetics" to explain how genes and environmental factors work together to determine an organism's observable traits and characteristics. This is a vital and increasingly recognized field of study that explores how environmental factors can affect the way genes are expressed, without altering the underlying DNA sequence. This field of study is particularly significant as it impacts the understanding of genetic and biological heritage and the complexities of genetics, biology, and familial relationships.

In epigenetics, one of the key areas of interest is how trauma can influence genetic expression. Research suggests that traumatic experiences, including those of previous generations, can lead to epigenetic changes that can be passed down to offspring. This has profound implications for individuals in the genetic continuity loss community, as it suggests that the experiences of genetic parents and ancestors could have a lasting impact on their identity and health, even if they are not raised by their genetic family, and on future generations as well.

Epigenetics brings a new dimension to the concept of parenthood in assisted reproduction. When a recipient mother uses a donor egg, some fertility specialists propose that the act of carrying and delivering the baby, influenced by the mother's own body and environment, can lead to epigenetic changes in the child. The recipient mother exerts a biological influence on the child, despite not being the genetic parent. Woman are told they are therefore the 'biological' mother. This is why terms like 'genetic parent' is used rather than 'biological', as the latter is evolving to mean the role a woman has in the gestation of a child which may or may not include genetic material.

Understanding epigenetics is crucial as it expands the definition of biological connections beyond just the genetic code. It underscores the idea that our environments, behaviors, and experiences can be influential on who we are and our health. This is why raising parents' do have an impact on their children. This knowledge can provide comfort and a sense of biological connection to those who may not have a direct genetic link to their raising parents or children, adding a new layer of understanding to the complex tapestry of family and identity.

E

ethnicity shift

...is when a direct-to-consumer (DTC) DNA test indicates someone's ethnicity is significantly different from what they were raised to believe.

Envision a film titled "Trading Roots: A DNA Discovery" that centers around a character who experiences an ethnicity shift after a DTC DNA test. Similar to the role-reversal in "Trading Places", the protagonist finds their life turned upside down as they grapple with a newfound ethnic background, vastly different from their upbringing. The story humorously and thoughtfully explores themes of identity, cultural and familial connection, feelings of being an imposter, to eventually self-acceptance and belonging, as the character navigates this unexpected twist, learning to embrace and integrate their new heritage into their sense of self.

Trading Roots: A DNA Discovery (Trading Place)

An ethnicity shift can disrupt a person's sense of belonging leading to imposter feelings within both their raised culture and newfound ethnicity. The sense of continuity with one's roots is a vital aspect of personal identity, influencing connections to family history, traditions, cultural heritage, and a sense of belonging. This can be particularly impactful for adoptees or DCP who may be learning about their 'real' ethnicity for the first time or for those who have a significant shift in ethnicity from their original family narrative due to a DTC DNA test.

DTC DNA tests determine ethnicity by analyzing an individual's DNA and comparing it with their reference database that contains DNA samples from various populations. The accuracy of these tests depend on the representation of different populations in the database. Each company has a unique database, leading to varying estimates across different DTC DNA services. When they update their database, it may 'change' your ethnicity results.

When a person's test results reveal a significant divergence from what they were raised to believe, it can lead to complex emotional responses, including guilt and shame. Guilt from feeling like one doesn't have the lived experience of their 'new' ethnicity to claim it. Or from a sense of abandoning or neglecting the cultural traditions of the ethnic group they grew up in. Shame emerges from not knowing about the discrepancy in ethnicity, especially when family narratives reinforced an incorrect ethnic identity. People may feel 'dupped' by their family.

The *Right to Know 2021* survey revealed that more than half of the respondents reported ethnicities different from what they were raised to believe. For many, this shift had a profound impact on their self-perception and sense of belonging. These individuals often spent their lives trying to fit into a family identity that felt out of place. They may have felt accepted within their family unit but faced societal rejection or confusion when their claimed ethnicity did not align with societal expectations. The confirmation of a different ethnicity through a DNA test validated these feelings, offering a clearer understanding of their experiences and treatment by others.

An ethnicity shift often leads to a reevaluation of one's identity and heritage. Each individual's response to this discovery is unique and valid. You can choose to continue to identify with the ethnicity you grew up, or your new ethnicity, or both. This is deeply personal journey.

𝓕
fertility fraud

...is an intentional act of misrepresentation in assisted reproduction by medical professionals, clinics, or donors to recipient parents or donors.

In the high-stakes world of assisted reproduction, audiences journey through the underbelly of fertility clinics. Dr. BeFertile charms his way to the top of his profession with a potent mix of ambition, deception, and controversial practices. Behind the glossy facade of helping families grow, he navigates a murky world of ethical dilemmas, shortcuts, and personal gain. As the empire he built on lies begins to unravel, patients and colleagues alike start to question the origins of the miracles. The film weaves themes of trust, betrayal, and the quest for truth, transparency, and justice leaving viewers to ponder the true cost of creation in the age of modern medicine.

Jon Jones, 6'1", 186 lbs, blonde, green eyes, no medical issues, mom and dad living, only child, enjoys soccer.

The Wolf of Sperm Street (The Wolf of Wall Street)

Fertility fraud involves unethical practices in assisted reproductive, where trust between recipient parents and medical professionals is paramount. This involves deceptive practices by fertility doctors or other medical personnel, clinics, or donors. The deception can take various forms, but all lead to significant emotional, financial, and sometimes genetic consequences for the victims.

The most egregious form of fertility fraud occurs when a doctor uses his own sperm, without consent, to inseminate patients. Donors, sperm and egg, also misrepresent their educational, social, and medical background. There is an incentive to enhance their information so their specimen will be chosen. There are no verification requirements in the U.S.

Another form of fertility fraud involves the mishandling or mislabeling of genetic material. This can result in embryos or gametes (sperm or eggs) being switched, leading to a child genetically unrelated to one or both intended parents. Such incidents may arise from negligence, poor practices, or deliberate fraud within fertility clinics. Clinics also exaggerate success rates or the effectiveness of certain treatments, coercing patients into expensive and emotionally taxing procedures that may have little chance of success. Fraud also encompasses the commercial exploitation of surrogates and egg donors, often involving coercion, misinformation, or exploitation of economically disadvantaged women. This raises serious ethical concerns about consent, autonomy, and the commodification of human reproductive capabilities.

Fertility fraud represents a violation of the most fundamental aspects of trust and ethics in medicine. Patients should have access to accurate information about the procedures, the success rates of fertility clinics, and the backgrounds of donors. Parents and offspring should have ongoing access to medical information and the identity of the donor and siblings. We must foster a culture of ethical practice in assisted reproduction where success is not just the creation of a baby but where the welfare of patients and their future children is paramount.

Addressing fertility fraud will require enacting stringent federal regulatory oversight in the U.S., transparency, and accountability in assisted reproduction and ensuring that those who commit fertility fraud are held accountable.

𝓕

FOG (fear, obligation, and guilt/grief)

...is the process where individuals affected by adoption, assisted reproduction, or non-paternal events (NPEs) come to terms with their feelings and realizations about their loss of genetic continuity.

Individuals navigate a world where they've always accepted their familial narratives as reality. But, akin to Neo's journey in "The Matrix", they gradually awaken to their true genetic identities, challenging everything they've known. As they 'unplug' from their perceived histories, they embark on a life transforming journey of self-discovery. The film captures the profound, often emotional process of coming to terms with one's origins, mirroring the awakening from a life-long illusion like Neo to embrace a newfound reality.

The Genetic Matrix: Unplugged (The Matrix)

The acronym FOG was first coined by Susan Forward & Donna Frazier in their book *Emotional Blackmail*. The FOG, an acronym for Fear, Obligation, and Guilt/Grief, represents the emotional haze that can cloud one's understanding of their genetic identity and/or connection. Coming out of the FOG occurs in phases as awareness emerges and individuals affected by adoption, assisted reproduction, or non-paternal events (NPEs) confront, process, and resolve the impact of loss of genetic continuity on their lives.

Coming out of the FOG is about seeking validation and understanding, recognizing that the emotions and behaviors one exhibits may stem from deep-seated roots tied to their conception or adoption, relinquishment of a child, or loss of genetic connection to one or both parents. Amy Barker, LMHC and Jennifer Joy Phoenix, LSWAIC, with *Adoption Savvy* have developed FOG Fazes for those impacted by these events. People often begin with disengaging, where they are detached from the implications of their genetic origins. As they move through denying and defending, they protect themselves from the potential pain of exploring these roots. Eventually, they begin discerning and questioning the narratives they've been told and acknowledging the impact their genetic identity and lack of genetic mirroring has had on their life.

The next stages involve a deeper exploration and emotional reckoning. Deconstructing long-held beliefs, drowning in the overwhelming flood of emotions and questions, and developing a new understanding of their identity. It's a period marked by grief, anger, and, sometimes, reconciliation as one navigates through reunion attempts and reshapes their self-perception.

The final stage—deciding—marks the emergence of a new identity, where individuals integrate their past with their present and future. It's a reclamation of autonomy, where shame and confusion give way to validation and pride. Here, one establishes healthier relationships, communicates needs effectively, and embraces both the culture they were raised in and the one they are genetically tied to.

For those who have a DNA surprise, the phases of awareness and development are similar, but the emotional impact can be more intense. Coming out of the FOG is about moving from a place of obscured truths to a space of clear, autonomous self-identity.

60

g

genetic attraction (GA)

...is when close genetically related individuals who were separated meet later in life and experience a strong emotional and/or physical attraction to each other.

In a take on "Lost in Translation", we explore the nuanced reality of genetic attraction. This film portrays individuals who, after being separated and then reunited with close genetic relatives, experience intense, confusing emotions often mistaken for romantic feelings. The story delves into their inner turmoil and self-awareness journey, much like the characters in "Lost in Translation" grappling with their complex bond. It sensitively navigates the fine line between deep familial connection and societal taboos, highlighting the importance of understanding these natural emotions and the need for open dialogue.

Natural Attraction: The Genetic Bond (Lost in Translation)

Genetic attraction is a natural, often misunderstood phenomenon that occurs when individuals who are closely genetically related but have been separated reunite. According to Leslie Pate Mackinnon LCSW, reunion can evoke intense emotional or physical reactions, sometimes mistaken for romantic feelings due to their similarity to sensations experienced in dating or falling in love. Recognizing this natural occurrence can help individuals navigate these feelings responsibly, avoiding taboo directions.

When we first enter into reunion we want to impress our new relative. Before meeting, we often dress up to ensure we look nice. We wait for their calls or texts. There is a lot of time, connection, and experience we are trying to make up for.

Genetic attraction can be confusing and overwhelming. It's often driven by a lack of shared childhood experiences or familial bonds growing up, leading to intense, mislabeled emotions upon entering into reunion. This attraction might manifest as an inexplicable pull towards the other person due to the synchronicities you see and feel both literally (in appearance, body language, speech patterns) and personality and intellectually. There is often a desire or need for physical closeness to make up for lost time and connectivity. Some people revert to their childhood self as people regress to their development stages which may have been truncated due to separation. People also experience an emotional bond with this new 'Intimate Stranger' that feels deeper than you would expect from someone you just met.

The confusion lies in the interpretation of these feelings, which if misunderstood, can lead to discomfort or inappropriate relationships. It's crucial for individuals to be aware of genetic attraction and its potential impacts. This way, when these feeling arise, you understand where they are coming from. Open lines of communication with your new family member is important. Counseling and open discussions about this possibility before entering into reunion is encouraged. We need more research here and on all impacts associated with loss of genetic continuity.

Genetic attraction, while complex, highlights the profound impact of genetics and attachment on human relationships. It underscores the importance of emotional preparation and support for those deciding to reunite with genetic relatives. Recognizing and respecting the boundaries of these relationships is essential for a healthy reunion and ongoing relationships.

_g_
genetic bewilderment

...is growing up genetically unrelated to one or both of your parents and feeling out of place but not knowing why.

"The Sixth Sense of Self" delves into the inner world of a protagonist experiencing genetic bewilderment. Similar to the young boy in "The Sixth Sense" who can see ghosts, the main character slowly consciously realizes they are not genetically related to their family. This revelation, akin to seeing an unseen world, leads them on a journey of self-discovery. The film portrays their emotional and psychological struggles as they come to terms with their identity and loss of genetic mirroring echoing the suspense and revelation in the original film. It's a gripping tale of coming to understand one's true self in a world that is not as it seemed.

The Sixth Sense of Self (The Sixth Sense)

63

The concept was first introduced in a 1952 letter by psychiatrist E. Wellisch to the Journal of Mental Health. The term 'genealogical bewilderment' was later coined by his colleague psychologist H. J. Sants in 1964 who wrote about the problems of children who have uncertain, little, or no knowledge of one or both of their genetic parents. Genetic bewilderment affects those who are adopted, donor-conceived, or who have an NPE.

At its core, genetic bewilderment is rooted in the absence of genetic mirroring—the inability to see one's physical, emotional, or behavioral traits reflected in your family members. For many, this leads to a persistent feeling of being out of place, often described as monachopsis or feeling like the 'black sheep' in the family. This can manifest as a subtle, lingering doubt about one's belonging in the family, which might be dismissed or overlooked in childhood but becomes more pronounced with age.

The discovery of true genetic origins can be shocking for individuals, leading to a profound sense of betrayal, especially if this information was deliberately withheld from them. This revelation often reshuffles a person's understanding of family history and their identity, causing them to question their place within their family and the broader world. They might grapple with questions about their genetic parents, their cultural heritage, and the reasons behind their conception or adoption.

This sense of bewilderment can have significant emotional consequences, including feelings of loss, anger, and grief. The loss is not only about the genetic parent they never knew but also about the loss of a certain understanding of their identity and childhood and familial history. There is also a mourning for the familial bonds they thought they had, which can strain relationships with their raising family members.

Understanding and addressing genetic bewilderment is crucial for the emotional well-being of individuals dealing with these complex issues. It underscores the importance of openness and honesty in conversations about genetic heritage within families, which should begin when a child is non-verbal. Navigating genetic bewilderment often requires emotional support, such as counseling, support groups, or therapy.

g

genetic continuity loss community

...is individuals united by the shared experience of the absence of relationships with genetic parents and children during the child's upbringing.

This film follows the tenacious rallying of the Genetic Continuity Loss Community. Together, they confront the veil of secrecy to reclaim their genetic narratives and ties. In this journey of identity and belonging, individuals face the heartache of unknown origins and the longing to connect with genetic roots and family. This tale highlights the collective struggle for truth and transparency and the deep-seated desire to know your genetic family from both the parent and child perspectives. It's a poignant exploration of family, identity, and the unbreakable bonds forged in the quest for answers and the right to know your genetic history and family.

Erin Brockovich: Genes Unearthed (Erin Brockovich)

The genetic continuity loss community encompasses a broad spectrum of individuals bound together by the common thread of disrupted or absent genetic parent-child connections during a child's upbringing. This community is not limited to a single scenario but spans across adoption, assisted reproduction, and NPEs, each presenting its unique challenges and experiences but with overlapping commonalities. The ramifications of genetic discontinuities extend far beyond the immediate parent-child relationship, rippling through the entire constellation of connected lives.

At the heart of this community are the individuals directly impacted: the children (who may now be adults) such as DCP, adoptees, and those with an NPE (first-degree people). Their experiences of identity, belonging, and connection are profoundly shaped by the absence or alteration of genetic ties. Surrounding them are the genetic parents—those who have contributed genetically but may not be present in the child's life. And there are the raising parents, who provide the day-to-day care, love, and support, irrespective of genetic linkage.

The impact does not stop with these immediate relationships. Significant others and the children of the first degree individuals often navigate the complex emotional and psychological landscapes that come with such family dynamics. Siblings, whether fully, half, or not at all genetically related, also play roles in this intricate web, influencing and being influenced by the core issues of genetic continuity loss.

The extended family, encompassing both genetic and raising relatives, and even close friends, are integral to the broader network of relationships. They too are touched by the nuances of these connections, contributing to and being affected by the overall family narrative.

This term aims to provide an inclusive umbrella that acknowledges the diversity and complexity of experiences within these groups. It recognizes that the journey of understanding, acceptance, and integration of these unique familial constructs involves not just the individuals at its core but a wider circle of connected lives. This term is indeed a work in progress, reflecting the ongoing dialogue and nascent information about these groups and the impacts of loss of genetic continuity. Perhaps a more concise term will develop over time.

g

genetic identity

...is your unique set of genetic characteristics and traits inherited from your genetic parents that contributes to your physical appearance, health, and aspects of your personality, likes, and behavior.

Throughout this film, a series of life events and revelations lead both mother and son to realize just how similar they are, not just in appearance but also in personality and behavior. The narrative weaves through their individual and shared experiences, highlighting the powerful influence of genetic inheritance in shaping their preferences, talents, personalities, likes, and professional choices much like the comedic yet insightful journey in "Freaky Friday". This heartwarming story underscores the undeniable bond, synchronicities, and surprising parallels within family genetics.

Freaky Genetics: Like Mother Like Son
(Freaky Friday)

The concept of 'genetic personhood' delves into the philosophical, ethical, and genetic aspects of what constitutes a person and how this intersects with cultural, social, and ethical perspectives. Genetic identity is intricately connected to one's health, personality, and familial bonds and plays a crucial role in shaping who we are. Knowing your genetic identity is privilege and it should be a right. Read *Blueprint: How DNA Makes Us Who We Are* by Robert Plomin for more on the role of genetics.

The surge in popularity of DTC DNA tests has brought to light the complexities of genetic identity. These tests can uncover a person's true genetic origins, leading to unexpected discoveries that significantly impact emotional well-being, family dynamics, and your medical care and a greater understanding you.

A critical aspect of understanding genetic identity are the implications for medical health. Knowledge of genetic makeup can reveal predispositions to certain diseases, enabling individuals to take preventive measures or seek early treatment. Conversely, misconceptions about one's genetic heritage can lead to inappropriate health decisions, delayed diagnoses, or unnecessary medical interventions. This not only places a financial burden on individuals and the healthcare system but also impacts the mental health of those affected. Knowing one's genetic relatives is essential for understanding physical and behavioral traits and avoiding romantic relationships with close relatives, a concern very relevant in assisted reproduction.

There is an emerging consensus on the importance of codifying genetic identity rights. This movement emphasizes the need for transparency in birth certificates, adoption records, and assisted reproduction practices. Legal recognition ensures that individuals have access to crucial information about their genetic identity, enabling them to make informed decisions about their health, understand their identity and heritage, and navigate familial relationships with greater clarity.

This is not just a matter of genetic inheritance; it's a cornerstone of personal and social identity, deeply intertwined with health, cultural heritage, and family dynamics. As society grapples with the implications of new genetic technologies, the conversation around genetic identity rights is increasingly pertinent, highlighting the need for ethical considerations and legal frameworks to support individuals in their fundamental human right to know their genetic identity.

g
genetic mirroring

...is seeing your physical characteristics, talents, psychological tendencies, likes, and emotional patterns reflected in your family members.

The "Identity Trap" revolves around a character discovering their genetic family at age 48. The theme song for their life is "One of These Things" from Sesame Street. Much like the twins in "The Parent Trap" who are amazed by their synchronicities upon meeting, the protagonist here experiences a series of revelatory moments of genetic mirroring when they meet their newfound genetic relatives. The film explores the emotional journey of self-discovery, the joy of finding physical, psychological, and emotional traits mirrored in others, and the profound sense of connection and belonging that comes from these newfound family ties.

The Identity Trap (The Parent Trap)

69

Genetic mirroring is a fundamental aspect of human development and identity formation, referring to the recognition of oneself in the physical, emotional, and behavioral traits of family members. This natural process of seeing similarities in facial features, personality traits, and even talents within a family aids individuals, especially children, in forming a sense of belonging and self-understanding.

For example, a child might notice they share the same laugh as their mother or the same artistic talent as their father. These shared characteristics reinforce their identity and familial bond. Genetic mirroring extends beyond physical resemblances to include mannerisms, interests, speech patterns, professional choices, and even certain responses to situations, contributing to a deeper sense of connection and continuity within the family unit.

Individuals who are raised in families where they are not genetically related to one or both of their parents may face challenges due to a lack of genetic mirroring. Because they do not see their traits or behaviors reflected in their family members this leads to feelings of disconnection or confusion about their identity. For instance a LDDCP may question why they are the only one in the family with a passion for fixing things, an LDA might wonder why they don't physically resemble anyone in their family, or someone with an NPE may wonder why they are nothing like their father.

This absence of genetic mirroring can sometimes result in self-esteem issues, insecurity, and feelings of being the "black sheep" or out of place. The realization or suspicion of not being genetically related to their family can be particularly jarring, leading to an identity crisis and feelings of isolation, which can affect an individual's development and well-being. This can also lead to genetic bewilderment.

It is therefore important to inform children from birth if they are not genetically related to one or both of their raising parents. Being aware of this from a young age can help a child understand why they might feel different. With this knowledge, they can grow in a manner that is healthy and informed, mitigating potential issues related to genetic mirroring and bewilderment.

g

genetic (bio/birth/first) parent
genetic (bio/birth/first) mother (BMom)
genetic (bio/birth/first) father (BF)

...is a person's genetic father or mother, sometimes referred to biological, bio, birth, first, or natural mother or father (or parent).

It's your own version of "Mamma Mia", but it's less about a picturesque Greek island and ABBA songs, and more about a whirlwind journey through DNA tests and ancestry sites to find your genetic parent(s). Who knew your life would turn into a quest to find your genetic family and your sense of self. This movie is complete with plot twists and unexpected discoveries. Maybe you should start practicing your dance moves—it's your own version of "Dancing Queen" meets genealogy. Wonder if there's a song for that!

DNA Mia! The Search for My Dancing Genetics (Mama Mia)

Parents often wonder why adjectives like 'genetic,' 'bio,' 'birth,' or 'first' are necessary prefixes to the word 'parent.' These terms become essential when distinguishing between multiple parental figures in a person's life. Importantly, these descriptors are neutral; they don't carry any inherent positive or negative connotations. For example, in families with raising parents, genetic parents, and stepparents, referring to 'my real parent' can be ambiguous. Precise descriptors help clarify to whom someone is referring.

An inherent bond exists between a child and their genetic parents, a connection that remains unbreakable. When a child is separated from their genetic family, they subconsciously sense this loss, potentially leading to what's known as a primal wound. Acknowledging this bond and loss is crucial in helping children cope with and heal from the trauma of separation.

Children possess a remarkable ability to love and form strong attachments. They naturally bond with caregivers who show them love and support, this is a child's real parent. But this does not diminish their desire or need to connect with their genetic parents and family. Recognizing that a child can love all their parental figures is vital.

When children are informed about their genetic identity from an early age, they are often better equipped to handle the knowledge of their origins. This early awareness can reduce the potential for trauma, as it addresses their innate curiosity and the biological need to understand their identity and to know where they come from.

Understanding and respecting the various parental roles is critical for a child's psychological development and well being. Open discussions and acknowledgment of these diverse relationships create a healthier emotional environment. This approach aids children in comprehending and integrating their complex family dynamics, fostering a sense of wholeness and acceptance.

No one should dictate to a person the terms they should use when referring to their parents. Some people choose to use different terms and this should be respected by everyone in the family. And what terms someone chooses to use my evolve over time.

g
genetic recombination

...is the exchange of genetic material that leads to children with different combinations of DNA that can differ from in each sibling.

We delve into a narrative that echoes Alan Turing's mission to decode the complex, paralleling this with the intricate 'genetic codes' that dictate siblings' diverse traits as this film echoes 'The Imitation Game' . The story, set within a large family, reveals the unique journey of each sibling, illustrating that, despite common parentage, they each harbor distinct traits. This exploration illuminates the mysterious and unpredictable nature of inheritance. Echoing Turing's breakthroughs, the film presents nature's own cryptographic challenge, showcasing the elaborate and varied mosaic of each life as a testament to the unforeseen splendor of genetics.

The Combination Game (The Imitation Game)

73

Genetic recombination is a biological process where chromosomes exchange DNA segments during cell division, particularly in the formation of eggs and sperm. This exchange leads to new gene combinations, differing from those in either parent, and is fundamental to sexual reproduction, contributing significantly to genetic diversity.

A key outcome of genetic recombination is its role in determining genetic similarities and differences among siblings with the same genetic parents. Due to the random mixing of parental chromosomes, each sibling inherits a unique gene set. While they share genetic similarities, there are also distinct differences between them.

This variation is evident in the measurement of shared centiMorgans (cMs), units describing the length of DNA segments shared between relatives. The amount of DNA siblings share, influenced by genetic recombination, can significantly differ. Typically, full siblings share about 50% of their DNA, but this can range from 1,613 to 3,488 cMs, underscoring each individual's unique genetic identity. This is why a child with a mom who is 100% French and a dad who is 100% Chinese can have one child that is 45% French and 55% Chinese and another child that is 40% French and 60% Chinese.

An analogy to understand this is to compare it to a pot of stew that represents the parents. The stew contains carrots, peas, potatoes, celery, and beef (different DNA segments). When you ladle the stew into one bowl, you might get a few vegetables, lots of potatoes, and some meat. The next bowl might have fewer potatoes, more meat, and a greater variety of vegetables. Despite starting with the same pot, each bowl has a different combination of ingredients. This is akin to genetic recombination, where the same 'ingredients' from parents combine differently in each child.

Genetic recombination can be influenced by 'junk DNA' or 'dark DNA' which makes up approx. 98% of the human genome. Dark DNA, despite not encoding proteins, contains regions that can be involved in regulatory functions, structural aspects of chromosomes, and the facilitation of genetic processes that can impact how genes are recombined and expressed. The interplay between non-coding DNA and genetic recombination is an area of investigation. Research shows the minimal impact our raising environment has on who we are.

g
ghostkingdom

...is a hypothetical world adoptees, DCP, NPE individuals, and parents enter when imagining being part of their genetic family or raising their genetic child.

Here predicting the future is replaced with revealing different variations of the past. Adoptees, DCP, NPE individuals, and parents access a technology that allows them to explore various scenarios of their lives had they grown up with their genetic families or raised their genetic child. Similar to the precognitive themes in "Minority Report", the protagonists confront multiple "echoes" of their past, each revealing different facets of identity. This exploration into the 'ghostkingdom' of alternate pasts offers a compelling look at the impact of family, genetics, and the choices that shape our lives.

Majority Report: Echoes of Yesterday
(Minority Report)

The term Ghostkingdom was coined by author Jean Strauss in her book *Birthright: The Guide to Search and Reunion for Adoptees, Birthparents, and Adoptive Parents* and is a psychological concept often experienced by adoptees, DCP, and people with an NPE. It represents an imaginary realm where these individuals envision an alternate life with their genetic family. This hypothetical world allows them to ponder 'what could have been', exploring scenarios of growing up with or being part of their genetic family.

Some genetic parents who relinquished a child or who donated gametes or an embryo may also experience their own ghostkingdom imaging what it would have been like to raise their child. Raising parents also visit their ghostkingdom where they are genetically related to their child(ren). Siblings or other family members also have a ghostkingdom too.

Visiting a ghostkingdom can be a therapeutic exercise, providing a space for individuals to process feelings of loss, curiosity, or longing for connections they never had. It offers a way to understand and come to terms with their unique life stories, especially in understanding the impact of not being raised by genetic parents or raising genetic children. In the beginning of a DNA surprise or reunion, we may visit our ghostkingdom more often to help process through our discovery. We may return later during milestones in our lives.

While spending time in this imagined reality can be beneficial for emotional processing, it is also important to find balance. Prolonged dwelling in the ghostkingdom can impede living in the present and moving forward. Individuals are encouraged to use these reflections as a means to gain insight and perhaps closure but also to focus on the realities of their current lives and relationships.

It is crucial to acknowledge and appreciate the life we have lived, the relationships we have formed, and the person we've have become. This involves creating and embracing the experiences, both in genetic and non-genetic families, and integrating these into a sense of self and new world view. Moving forward from the ghostkingdom means building a life that acknowledges the past but is not defined by it. This allows for the formation of meaningful connections and to pursue aspirations in the here and now.

g
guardianship

...is a legal process empowering a caregiver with the decision-making authority for a child without officially severing the genetic parents' connection to the child.

Imagine a world where the Witness Protection Program is repurposed to safeguard not just identities but the very essence of familial bonds in "Preserver". Here the protagonist, armed with the ability to 'erase' the bureaucratic red tape, becomes the unsung hero for children whose parents cannot care for them to ensure they don't lose the thread to their roots. This guardian of guardianship deftly navigates the delicate balance between new beginnings and the indelible ink of heritage and familial connection, ensuring every child's story has both a safe harbor and an open book to their origins.

Preserver (Eraser)

Guardianship, within the adoption community, is a preferred alternative when kinship adoption isn't an option. This approach allows a child to maintain their original identity, as recorded on their birth certificate, without the need for modifications typically seen in traditional adoptions. In many ways, adoptees have likened the experience of adoption to being placed in a witness protection program, where their names, and potentially their birth dates and places, are altered, obscuring their original identities. Guardianship, however, offers a different path (as would significant birth certificate reform).

Under guardianship arrangements, a person(s) is legally appointed to provide care and make decisions on behalf of the child, much like adoptive parents. However, unlike adoption, guardianship does not require the issuance of a new birth certificate. The child's name, birth date, and place of birth remain unchanged, preserving their connection to their genetic heritage. This continuity is crucial for many in the adoption community, as it allows individuals to retain a sense of personal history and identity.

For children and their guardians, this means that the legal ties to genetic parents remain intact, providing a clear understanding of their origins. This transparency is significant for many reasons, not least of which includes the preservation of medical history, cultural heritage, and the potential for future reunification or contact with genetic relatives.

Guardianship is particularly appealing for those who value the importance of knowing one's roots. It offers a solution that respects the child's original identity while ensuring their safety, care, and well-being under the guardianship of committed caregivers. This approach aligns with the growing recognition of the importance of maintaining connections to one's genetic heritage, addressing concerns within the adoption community about identity erasure and loss of connection to genetic roots.

Guardianship presents a compassionate alternative within the adoption spectrum, prioritizing the child's right to their personal history and identity and this gives the care provider the ability to make legal decisions for the child. It acknowledges the complex emotions and needs of adoptees, offering a pathway that respects their origins while ensuring their future well-being under the care of dedicated guardians.

ℋ
hiraeth

...is a deep sense of longing for a home, a place, or a time that may never have existed, or that one cannot return to.

Similar to Dorothy's longing for Kansas in the "Wizard of Oz", this narrative delves into the profound emotion of hiraeth. The story follows a character on a metaphorical journey, seeking a sense of belonging and home in a world that feels both familiar and elusive. Along the way, they encounter various scenarios symbolizing their deep nostalgia and yearning for a sense of home or time that may never have existed, echoing Dorothy's realization that "there's no place like home". The film combines a sense of adventure with introspection, exploring the universal quest for connection and the places we call home in our hearts.

Home: The Journey Within (The Wizard of Oz)

Hiraeth, a deeply evocative Welsh term, embodies a complex mixture of longing, nostalgia, and wistfulness, often for a home or a place to which one cannot return, or that may never have existed. It's not just homesickness but a soul-deep yearning for belonging, for connection, for a place in the world that feels intrinsically right and familiar.

For many adoptees, donor-conceived people, and individuals who experience an NPE, hiraeth is a poignant and familiar sentiment. It encapsulates their longing for a home they never knew, a family they were never part of, and a heritage they may have been separated from. This yearning isn't just for a physical place but for the sense of identity and belonging that comes from being connected to one's origins. It's a longing for answers to the unspoken questions about who they are and where they come from.

They might feel hiraeth as a desire to connect with their genetic roots or a longing for the life they might have lived had circumstances been different. People sometimes visit their ghostkingdom to alleviate some of their hiraeth feelings. It's also a yearning to understand the missing pieces of their identity, to have genetic mirroring—see their traits and characteristics reflected in a genetic relative, and to feel a sense of genetic continuity.

For those who discover through a DNA surprise that their familial understanding is not what they thought, hiraeth can take on a bittersweet quality. They might long for the simplicity and innocence of their life before the discovery, for the comfort of a home that felt like theirs before their perception of it was irrevocably altered. It's a longing to return to a sense of self before their world was upended. Or if they felt like they never quite fit in with their raising family, it may be a longing for a home where they feel fully accepted and a strong innate sense of belonging.

Hiraeth in these contexts is more than just a feeling; it's a journey of the soul towards understanding and reconciliation with one's past. It's a deep-seated part of the human quest for identity and belonging, resonating profoundly with those whose life experiences have left them with unanswered questions about their place in the world.

g

imposter syndrome

...is someone with a misattributed parentage experience who feels like an impostor in the family/ethnicity they were raised in and/or their newly discovered genetic family/ethnicity.

"The Imposter: Unveiled Origins" explores the protagonist's emotional and psychological struggle in grappling with their newfound genetic identity. This discovery leads them down a path of questioning and reevaluating their life, family relationships, and cultural heritage. Mirroring the themes of uncertainty and mistaken identity in "The Imposter", here the protagonist faces the challenge of reconciling their past with the shocking new reality of their genetic origins. The film combines elements of mystery, drama, and a profound exploration of self-identity, heritage, family, and truth.

The Imposter: Unveiled Origins (Imposter)

Impostor syndrome encapsulates the profound emotional turmoil one experiences upon discovering a significant discrepancy between their believed and actual genetic identity. This revelation often triggers feelings of being an impostor within their own family (and ethnicity/heritage) and their new genetic family (and ethnicity/heritage), leading to a deep sense of disconnection and a questioning of their place in both their cultural and familial landscape.

These feelings can emerge when individuals learn that their parentage is not what they believed, or through DNA testing that they belong to a different ethnic background than they were raised to believe. Such discoveries can fundamentally shake one's understanding of their identity and belonging, causing them to feel like outsiders in their own lives and skin. The impact is not just emotional but also relational, as it can change family dynamics, birth order, and how one relates to their cultural heritage they were raised in.

The journey to reconcile this newfound genetic identity with their lived experiences and the narrative they grew up with is often challenging. It involves navigating a complex maze of emotions, including guilt, shame, confusion, trepidation, and a profound sense of loss. This emotional journey can be likened to grieving the loss of one's assumed identity and familial connections while simultaneously trying to embrace and integrate a new one without fully feeling like you belong anywhere.

These feelings are further complicated by the reactions and acceptance of both their genetic and raised families and society. The struggle to find acceptance and a sense of belonging in either or both families can intensify feelings of being an impostor. It requires not only a redefinition of self-identity but also a renegotiation of relationships and roles within these family structures. Society also places expectations about who they are now allowed to publicly claim they are.

Dealing with impostor syndrome in the wake of DNA surprise involves a gradual process of acceptance, self-discovery, and rebuilding who you want to be. It calls for a compassionate understanding of one's emotions, open communication with family members, and in many cases, professional counseling to navigate the complex emotional landscape that arises from such profound revelations about one's identity.

g

intimate stranger

...is a newly discovered close genetic relative you only just met but you have an intrinsic connection.

In this cosmic drama of identity and connection, characters embark on a journey much like that of Luke Skywalker and Princess Leia in the new movie "Galactic Revelations Paradox." Adoptees, DCP, and individuals with an NPE experience a galaxy of emotions when they encounter intimate strangers, mirroring the Skywalker siblings' initial bond of instant familiarity and subsequent shock upon discovering their familial ties. This narrative explores the complex universe of connections, where people have an instant affinity for close relatives even from the first meeting due to shared genetics, leading to a redefinition of self and family, akin to the pivotal twist in the Star Wars saga.

Galactic Revelations Paradox (Star Wars V: Empire Strikes Back)

Adoptees, donor-conceived people, and individuals who experience an NPE and their close genetic relatives often experience the feeling of being intimate strangers when meeting as adults. This term describes the profound and immediate bond felt upon meeting for the first time, a close relative who, despite being a stranger in the conventional sense, shares an intrinsic and powerful link with the individual due to shared genetics.

Central to this phenomenon is the concept of genetic mirroring. When individuals encounter someone who shares their genetic makeup, there's often an instinctive recognition or sense of familiarity. This could manifest in physical resemblances, shared mannerisms and speech patterns, or similar interests and dispositions. For many, this encounter is profoundly impactful, as it might be the first time they see themselves reflected in another person in such a tangible way.

The emotional depth of these meetings cannot be overstated. For those who have grown up without knowledge or contact with genetic family members, meeting their relative - the intimate stranger - fills a void. It's not merely about seeing a familiar face, it's about connecting with a part of themselves that was previously unknown or missing. This connection often sparks a journey of self-discovery, reshaping their understanding of identity, belonging, connection, and family.

This phenomenon also brings complexity. It is important to remember the possibility of genetic attraction. And the initial euphoria of connection that may evolve into a nuanced relationship, as the realities of integrating this newly family member into one's life become apparent. The beginning of reunion is often referred to as the 'honeymoon phase', which then moves into a possible 'hangover', then limbo, and finally maintenance. The best advice for a successful reunion is to go slowly and have clear boundaries.

The intimate stranger phenomenon can bring to light questions about heritage, the meaning of family, and the nature of personal identity. And, it underscores the intricate interplay between genetics and social relationships, revealing how our understanding of ourselves and our place in the world can be profoundly altered by a single encounter.

ℳ

medical history

...is the record of heritable physical and mental health conditions essential to assess personal health risks and to develop a healthy lifestyle.

In "My Genetic Keeper" the Fitzgerald family faces a bewildering medical crisis: their daughter Kate battles an illness, previously unknown in their family history. As the plot thickens, a startling revelation emerges – Brian, Kate's devoted father, learns his father isn't who he thought. This casts a new light on Kate's illness, highlighting the critical importance of an accurate medical history. In their quest for answers the Fitzgeralds confront the ethical maze of who's entitled to family medical information. The true treasure isn't a legal battle or medical miracle, but the unveiling of Brian's genetic heritage, which holds the key to Kate's health and the power to redefine their relationships.

My Genetic Keeper (My Sister's Keeper)

In the context of the genetic continuity loss community, 'medical history' takes on a unique and crucial significance. Heritable family medical history refers to the comprehensive record of known health information, illnesses, conditions, and treatments that are genetically linked and inherited within a genetic family. This includes, but is not limited to, genetic disorders, chronic diseases, mental health conditions, and any hereditary traits that impact health.

We usually have access to this information through our parents. It is often as we age, that we start to pay attention to this information due to the development of our own medical conditions. When you don't know who your genetic parents are you can't ask them, "Did anyone in the family have a goiter."

For people who are misattributed, where they don't know they aren't related to one or both of their raising parents, medical history is huge issue. People base their health habits on their parents' medical history which could, if incorrect, lead to medical conditions that might have been prevented, delays in diagnosis, or unnecessary medical procedures. Slow diagnosis due to lack of information may lead to death or longterm health problems that could have been avoided. Unnecessary procedures, office visits, and surgeries may be performed due an accurate medical history. Not knowing true medical history adds a burden on individual's health and the health care system.

Merely possessing one's DNA information is not sufficient for a complete understanding of health risks and predispositions. Genetic counselors emphasize the need for a comprehensive family medical history to determine whether genetic markers, like the BRCA gene, will manifest into health issues. For example, the presence of the BRCA gene may be less concerning in individuals with no family history of cancer compared to those with multiple relatives who have had the disease.

Our current technology and understanding of genetics do not allow us to rely solely on DNA data; the context provided by family medical history is indispensable. This lack of a complete medical history in the genetic continuity loss community underlines the necessity of knowing one's genetic family's health background from birth in order to make informed healthcare decisions and risk assessments.

ℳ

misattributed parentage experience (MPE)

...is the discovery of a change in a person's perceived parental genealogy from an NPE, Adoption, or Assisted Reproduction.

"Operation, Who's Your Daddy" is centered around MPEs. The story follows the journey of two sisters who, have a DNA surprise and go in search of their father only to uncover the surprising truth about their parentage. Similar to the quest for paternal identity in "Father Figures", the sisters in this narrative embark on an emotional and sometimes humorous journey to identify their father only to uncover there's way more to their story—their mom's also not their mom. The film combines elements of self-discovery, family dynamics, and the complexities of genetic relationships, exploring the impact of these revelations on personal identity and family bonds.

Operation: Who's Your Daddy (Father Figures)

A misattributed parentage experience (MPE) is a revelation that upends one's understanding of their familial roots, sense of belonging, and identity. It occurs when an individual discovers they are not genetically related to one or both parents who raised them. This discovery often results from a direct-to-consumer (DTC) DNA test, which individuals undertake for various reasons, including curiosity about their ancestry.

'Misattributed' reflects the incorrect assignment of a person's genetic parentage. For some, an MPE reveals that the man they have known as their father is not genetically related to them from an affair, tryst, rape, assault, or other sexual encounter where paternity is obscured, hidden, or unknown, a situation commonly referred to as a non-paternal event (NPE). For others, it uncovers a late discovery of adoption (LDA) or the fact that they were conceived through assisted reproduction without their knowledge - late discovery donor-conceived person (LDDCP).

Colloquially an MPE is often referred to as having a DNA surprise (or as Not Parent Expected - NPE. Misattributed has been used by professionals in related fields (mental health, medical, genealogy) when assigned parentage is incorrect. By 1980, genetic counselors adopted the term "misattributed paternity" to describe cases when the person believed to be the father (presumed father) was discovered not to be the genetic father of a child. The legal profession began to utilize the term as well during the 1980s. In 1993, the term "misattributed parentage" was first used in genetic counseling, and by 2010, it was commonplace.

The use of parentage corresponds with the increased use of egg provision which doubled from 2000 to 2010. Non-profit organizations such as Right to Know use 'parentage' due to the possibility that it could be a mother or a father that is 'misattributed'. By 2019, genealogists started using "Misattributed Parentage Event." Now, the word 'experience' is often substituted for event to denote acknowledgment that this is not a "one time thing", but something someone will experience for the remainder of their life.

The number one word used to describe what people feel after having an MPE is shock, the next common feeling is validation and understanding of one sense of self. This is because people with an MPE often feel different from the rest of their family due to a lack of genetic mirroring and their MPE explains what they may have always sensed.

The emotional impact of an MPE is experienced on a spectrum from minor to profound and often triggers an identity crisis and reshapes one's sense of self and family. It can strain relationships within the raising family when individuals feel betrayed and angry from the secrets kept from them. Sometimes members of the family they grew up in reject them because they are no longer 'blood'. The repercussions extend to the nuclear family they have created, where spouses and children must grapple with the new reality and its implications for their shared identity and medical history.

In the wake of an MPE, individuals often engage with their 'ghostkingdom', the imagined lives they could have led if raised by their genetic families. While exploring these possibilities can be therapeutic, it is crucial for individuals to also embrace their present realities and the families they have known and formed. It's a delicate balance between reconciling with the past and forging a path forward with newfound knowledge and identity.

The MPE community includes LDAs, LDDCP, and individuals with an NPE. While their experiences may vary, common threads include:

- the loss of genetic continuity
- unknown or incorrect medical histories
- emotional turmoil of secret-keeping within families
- the commodification of ones origins
- societal gaslighting
- expected existential gratitude for your birth
- lack of genetic mirroring leading to genetic bewilderment
- identity crisis; and
- the process of identifying genetic family and deciding whether to reach out.

The discovery can lead to a search for genetic relatives and, potentially, to reunion fraught with emotional complexity. When someone has an MPE they face the decision of whether to search for their genetic family. A vast majority do decide to reach out. They want to see who they look like, would like their family medical history, family history information, and likely some level of a relationship. Reaching out is to new family takes bravery. Reunion, even a 'good' one, is challenging as there are a lot of emotions and the desire to make of for lost time. The best piece of advice is to go slow.

Reunion often starts out with a honeymoon phase, where everyone is on their best behavior and trying to get to know each other. Sometimes this followed by a possible 'hangover' if everyone dove in too fast. Then comes limbo where people may question if they want to continue with the relationship and to what degree and they're unsure what the other party wants. This is followed by the maintenance stage.

The antidote to the trauma of an MPE is connection. Connection can take different forms. Reaching out to others who've had an MPE is important so you understand you are not alone in what you are feeling. Keeping open communication with your significant other can help them understand what you're experiencing. If desired, continuing your usual interactions with the family you were raised in. And finally, talking with and continuing to build your relationship with your new family.

The societal shift towards recognition and the legitimization of diverse identities has prompted discussions around the terminology used to describe individuals with MPEs. Historically, terms like 'bastard' and 'illegitimate' carried stigma and legal disadvantages. Legal reforms and changing societal attitudes have since moved towards more neutral and less judgmental language, reflecting a broader understanding of family and identity.

As the language evolves, so too does the need for support structures for individuals navigating the aftermath of an MPE. Counseling, support groups, and community networks play a crucial role in helping individuals process their experiences and find solidarity with others who share similar stories.

Reducing societal shame and stigma from infertility, women's sexuality, and infidelity will give space to parents to have more candid discussions about a child's origins from the beginning as well as allow people to be more comfortable discussing their MPE so they can process and heal. It is estimated that 1 in 20 people have an MPE, translating to more than 16.6 million Americans. This figure underscores the importance of candid discussions about genetic identity and origins, as well as the need for more informed consent in the use of assisted reproduction, a restructuring of how we view and utilize adoption, and a shift in societal understanding of the need to know one's genetic identity from birth.

ℳ

monachopsis

...is the disconcerting and often persistent feeling of being out of place, even in familiar environments, creating a sense of disconnection from the surrounding world or the people in it.

In this underwater tale of identity and belonging, "The Siren's Dilemma" echoes the experiences of Ariel in "The Little Mermaid". This story mirrors her internal struggle, as she navigates through her aquatic realm filled with familiar faces and places, yet she is constantly drawn to the human world she perceives as her true belonging. The film delves into the emotional depth of feeling out of place in one's own environment, often due to a lack of genetic mirroring, highlighting the poignant journey towards identifying and building a place where one truly fits in the world.

The Siren's Dilemma (The Little Mermaid)

Monachopsis is the disconcerting feeling of being out of place, even in environments or social settings that should feel familiar. This concept is particularly resonant for adoptees, DCP, and individuals with an NPE, as these groups often grapple with issues of identity and belonging, making monachopsis a poignant aspect of their experiences.

For adoptees, this feeling can manifest as a sense of disconnection within their adoptive families or communities. Despite the presence of love and support, adoptees may still harbor a sense of not fully fitting, driven by a curiosity or longing for a connection to their genetic heritage. This feeling can become especially pronounced during familial gatherings or when surrounded by people who share a genetic link with each other but not with the adoptee.

DCP often encounter monachopsis in a unique way. They might grow up without knowledge of their donor-conceived status, or, if aware, not having access to information about their genetic parent(s). The revelation or awareness of being donor-conceived can induce a sense of dissonance, as their perceived identity may clash with newfound truths about their genetic origin. The feeling of being an 'outsider' in their own life story can be a common thread. Many LDAs and people with an NPE experience similar feelings.

Individuals who uncover an NPE face a similar emotional landscape. They might grow up with an intangible feeling of alienation, unable to pinpoint why they feel distinct from their family members. The feeling is akin to the sentiment expressed in the Sesame Street song 'One of These Things,' where they don't feel like they are like the other people in their family and they don't understand why not. This sensation of being the odd one out, without a clear understanding of the reason, can lead to deep-seated feelings of inadequacy or difference, further complicating their sense of self. Many LDDCP and LDAs might also feel as well.

Monachopsis encapsulates the complex emotional landscape of individuals navigating the intricate connections between genetics, family, and personal identity. It's a term that gives voice to a subtle, often unspoken feeling of alienation many feel, providing a language to describe an experience that is deeply personal and life changing.

N

name

...is a set of words by which a person is identified that often reflects aspects of personal identity, heritage, and cultural importance.

In "The Gene Redemption", you break into the vaults of your own genetic history. Picture yourself embarking on an epic quest, not unlike Andy Dufresne's escape, but this time, you're tunneling through ancestral databases and DNA records to uncover the truth of your origins and your ancestral name. As the plot unfolds, you unearth a long-lost genetic family. In a climactic homage to your newfound lineage, you choose to adopt a new name, symbolizing your liberation from the confines of uncertainty and embracing a new chapter in the lineage ledger. This is a renaissance of identity, where the final scene reveals the heritage you choose to claim.

The Gene Redemption (Shawshank Redemption)

Names hold profound significance across cultures and contexts, serving not just as identifiers but as vessels of identity, heritage, and personal narrative. They are the first and most enduring labels we receive, often imbued with meanings, expectations, and histories that shape our sense of self and our place in the world and our family.

In many cultures, names are more than mere tags; they are narratives in themselves, encapsulating personal traits, ancestral stories, or connections to the natural world. In these settings, names evolve with life's passages, reflecting milestones, achievements, or shifts in spiritual or social standing. Such practices underscore the belief that an individual's identity is interwoven with their community and environment, and that names should mirror this dynamic relationship.

Religious contexts further illuminate the importance of names, with traditions in Islam, Catholicism, Judaism, and other faiths treating name changes as markers of spiritual rebirth or commitment. These new names symbolize a departure from the past and an embrace of a new path, illustrating how names can encapsulate personal transformations and aspirations.

The act of taking a new name upon entering a monastic order or through marriage rituals highlights the role of names in signifying life transitions and new affiliations. These changes are not merely formalities but profound declarations of identity shifts and new beginnings.

The adoption of pseudonyms or stage names in professional realms reflects the multifaceted roles names play in shaping and expressing our identities. Such chosen names allow individuals to craft personas that resonate more closely with their self-perception or public image, showcasing the power of names to convey not just who we are, but who we aspire to be.

Names, therefore, are essential to our social fabric, acting as keys to our personal and collective stories, embodying our histories, relationships, and the pivotal moments that define us. The act of changing one's name can be a deeply personal and meaningful decision, reflecting a desire for change, growth, or new beginnings. After a DNA surprise or identifying your genetic family, some people choose to change their name. The ease of legally changing your name in the U.S. varies depending on in which state you reside.

𝒩

nature and nurture

...is the interplay between an individual's genetic inheritance and environmental influences in shaping their characteristics, development, preferences, and behaviors.

Here our leading lady raised amidst New York's skyscrapers uncovers that her roots trace back not to the concrete jungle but to the wide, open spaces of Texas. Her DNA surprise sends her spiraling into a world of cowboy boots and country roads, where she discovers a sister shaped under the Texan sun. Despite their different upbringings, the sisters find themselves eerily similar in quirks, laughter, and spirit, stirring up a comedic rodeo of nature versus nurture. This twist on "Twins" proves that while environment crafts the surface, the genetic blueprint sketches the soul proving family is can overcome different zip-codes.

Genetic Mirrors (Twins)

The interplay between nature and nurture in shaping human behavior and development has long been a subject of debate, especially for those in the adoption, assisted reproduction, and NPE communities. Robert Plomin, a prominent behavioral geneticist, offers compelling insights into this dialogue. His research suggests that while both genetic (nature) and environmental (nurture) factors contribute to individual differences, the influence of genetics prevails.

Our genetic makeup sets the boundaries within which environmental influences operate. It is our genes that lay the foundation for our potential, behaviors, and predispositions. For instance, a child's innate ability in mathematics might come from their genetic disposition, but how far they excel might be influenced by the educational opportunities they are provided.

Plomin argues that nurture is informed by nature. He introduces the concept of 'genetic nurture', where the environment's role is not merely passive but is actively shaped and chosen based on our genetic tendencies. This notion suggests that individuals naturally gravitate towards environments that complement and reinforce their genetic predispositions. For example, a person genetically inclined towards athleticism might seek out sports and physical activities, thereby creating a nurturing environment that aligns with their innate genetic proclivities.

This perspective has profound implications for understanding individual differences and the development of personality, intelligence, and mental health. It challenges the traditional dichotomy of nature versus nurture, proposing instead a more integrated approach that sees genes as central to shaping how we interact with our environment. This accounts for the synchronicities we see when close genetic relatives meet later in life for the first time.

For communities grappling with questions about identity and inheritance, Plomin's ideas offer a nuanced framework for understanding the complex interplay of genetic and environmental factors in human development. Recognizing the primary role of genetics in shaping who we are can provide a deeper understanding of the self and the multifaceted nature of human development and uphold why it is a fundamental human right to know your genetic identity form birth.

N

non-paternal event (NPE)

...is when someone is conceived from an extramarital affair, tryst, rape, assault, or other sexual encounter that results in hidden, undisclosed, or unknown paternity.

"Stellar Heritage: The Star-Lord Chronicles" is centered around an NPE where the protagonist has a strong bond with his raising father. The movie follows the journey of a man who discovers he is the offspring of a mysterious, secret affair, akin to Star-lord's revelation. In a twist, his father helps him find his genetic father and navigate reunion. Blending humor, adventure, and a bit of cosmic intrigue, the story explores the themes of identity, heritage, the father-child relationship, and the surprising turns life can take, all set against a backdrop of intergalactic discovery and bonds that transcend the ordinary.

The Tides of Healing (Guardians of the Galaxy)

An NPE, or Non-Paternal (Paternity) Event, is a term used to describe situations where an individual discovers that the person they have known as their father is not their genetic father. The genealogy community has used the term NPE in this context since around 2000. This discovery often comes as a shocking revelation, usually as a result of DTC DNA testing. It's a moment that can redefine someone's understanding of their identity, heritage, and the narrative of their family history. Colloquially people often use NPE to mean "Not Parent Expected" for someone who's had a DNA surprise (which would then also include LDAs and LDDCP too). Many professionals and organizations like Right to Know use the narrower definition in order to distinguish people with an NPE from donor-conceived individuals and adoptees.

Having an NPE tends to bring about profound emotional responses, including feelings of betrayal, confusion, anger, and shock. For the majority, learning this truth in adulthood adds a complex layer to their sense of self, familial relationships, and their relationship with their father. For some, the revelation brings them closer to their raising father. For others, it widens a gulf they didn't understand as a child but now makes sense. People must often decide if they wish to tell their raising father the truth about their origins if their mother didn't disclose this or didn't know. And this can lead to anxiety about the impact on their parents' relationship.

After the initial shock individuals with an NPE are faced with the challenge of reconstructing their identity and reevaluating their familial bonds. The desire for accurate records regarding paternity becomes a pressing issue, especially when the name on their birth certificate no longer represents their genetic lineage. The process of rectifying official documents to reflect genetic truth can be fraught with bureaucratic and emotional obstacles. In most states it is very difficult, and sometimes impossible to change your birth certificate even with a court order.

The journey of someone with an NPE is not just about grappling with the past; it's also about navigating the present and future with a new perspective on their genetic heritage and what family and fatherhood truly means. It's a path marked by the need for understanding, acceptance, and sometimes, the redefinition of relationships and personal history.

O

origin story

...is the foundational narrative of one's beginnings and heritage.

In "Echoes of Home," inspired by "Lion," the quest for one's origin story unfurls. Our protagonist, like Saroo, is adrift in a sea of unknown beginnings—his life a jigsaw with missing pieces. Armed with mere whispers of the past and the digital thread of modern technology, he embarks on a journey not just across the map, but into the depths of identity. This tale weaves a path back to his roots, where each step is a discovery, and every clue a beacon towards understanding his true self. It's a reminder that sometimes, to find where we truly belong, we must embark on a journey not outwards, but inwards, to the very heart of our origin. Knowing where we come from is the basis of our life story and the foundation of our future.

Echoes of Home (Lion)

Understanding one's origin story is a fundamental aspect of human identity and emotional well-being. For most people, the narrative of how they came into the world—where their parents met, the circumstances of their birth, and the lineage they hail from—is a given, a stable foundation upon which they build their sense of self and life story. However, for individuals who experience a DNA surprise, this foundational narrative is upended, leading to a profound sense of disorientation and the need to reconstruct their personal history.

A DNA surprise, such as discovering unexpected results from a DTC DNA test, can feel like the ground beneath you has turned to quicksand. Suddenly, the story you've been told about who you are and where you come from no longer aligns with the new information at hand. This revelation can shake the core of your identity, prompting a reevaluation of personal and familial relationships and a reassessment of your place in the world. Many feel untethered from their sense of self.

In this context, reconnecting with or discovering your origin story becomes a crucial step in the healing process. Knowing the specifics of your genetic heritage, such as where your genetic parents met or the circumstances surrounding your conception and birth, can provide a new foundation upon which to rebuild your identity. This knowledge can offer a sense of continuity and belonging, bridging the gap between the person you thought you were and the person you are discovering yourself to be.

The journey to uncover one's origin story can be complex and emotionally challenging, often involving difficult conversations and the navigation of sensitive family dynamics. Yet, it is through this journey that many find a path to healing. By piecing together the puzzle of their origins, individuals can begin to rewrite their personal narratives, integrating new information with the experiences and relationships that have shaped them. Ultimately, understanding your origin story is more than uncovering facts; it's about connecting with a deeper sense of identity and belonging. It's a privilege that, when disrupted by a DNA surprise, demands careful reconstruction. For those on this journey, rediscovering their origin story can be a vital step toward healing.

𝓟

primal wound

...is a deep and enduring emotional trauma that a child who's been separated from their genetic parent(s) at birth carries which with them and impacts their sense of identity, emotional well-being, and relationships.

This film centers on the journey of an individual overcoming separation trauma. Similar to Tom Hanks's character's isolation and eventual self-discovery on a deserted island, the protagonist in this narrative faces and heals from the deep-seated emotional pain of early separation from their genetic mother. The film explores themes of resilience, self-discovery, and the journey back to emotional well-being, mirroring the Chuck Noland's struggle to reconnect with the world and their own sense of identity after a life-altering separation.

The Tides of Healing (Castaway)

'The Primal Wound', a concept coined by Nancy Newton Verrier, delves into the emotional trauma experienced by children separated from their genetic mothers at birth. This concept extends to anyone in the genetic continuity loss community. It is not just an abstract theory; it's a palpable, deep-seated emotional injury that significantly influences one's sense of identity, emotional well-being, and interpersonal relationships.

For adoptees and DCP separated from their biological mothers, regardless of the circumstances or the age at which it occurs, this separation often leaves an indelible mark on their psyche. The bond between a genetic mother (and surrogate) and child is critical to psychological development and the formation of secure attachments. Children removed from their genetic mother must form their sense of identity without access to familial information and the benefits of genetic mirroring. And they have to try and develop attachments after their most fundamental bond was disrupted. This shaky foundation can manifest as feelings of abandonment, struggles with trust and attachment, and an ongoing search for a sense of belonging.

The primal wound can be particularly jarring for people who have a DNA surprise (LDA or LDDC) because a person's established identity and connections with their now raising mother are challenged leading to profound emotional upheaval and a reevaluation of personal history. The revelation that your dad isn't genetically related to you can shake the foundations of your identity and the relationship with the father who raised you. It raises complex questions about your place within the family and society, and can lead to feelings of betrayal and uncertainty about your lineage.

Genetic parents often carry their own emotional burden, particularly mothers, who may feel a deep sense of loss and grief. Fathers, too, can experience a sense of disconnection and loss, especially in NPE situations where they discover they are not the genetic parent or a genetic father who feels like they missed out on seeing their child grow up.

We must acknowledge that we cannot just substitute a new parent and the child will not notice the difference. Addressing the primal wound created from separation involves acknowledging the profound impact of genetic disconnections.

ℛ

raising child(ren)

...is an individual nurtured and brought up by a person who may or may not be genetically related.

Chaos and comedy ensue when two single parents, each with their own set of kids, unite their families and then welcome a daughter, Emma, together. Tragedy strikes when the mother dies in a car crash 13 years later, and the family learns she had relinquished a daughter, Laura, during the Baby Scoop Era. Emma, grappling with her new understanding of their mother—who was so loving and put all the children first— wonders how she could have given up Laura. Laura's grief over the loss of their mother is mitigated by Emma's stories filled with love, warmth, their mother's cooking adventures. Amidst the laughter and occasional mayhem, "Me, You, Ours" reveals that love, patience, and a sense of humor are key in blending lives and hearts.

Me, Your, Ours (Yours, Mine & Ours)

In the modern multifaceted realm of familial relationships, the concept of a 'raised child' emerges with particular significance, especially in the context of DNA surprises, adoption, assisted reproduction, and NPEs. A raised child is an individual brought up by a person or persons who may not share a genetic link. When someone reaches out to their new genetic parent(s), the child(ren) that person reared is their 'raised child(ren)'.

If you are adopted or donor conceived this is your genetic parent's child they raised, or if you had an NPE the child(ren) your genetic father raised. The child may not necessarily be genetically related but has the lived history with the parent. They can be a great resource to learn information about the new parent(s) and hold the emotional context of a family's journey. The raising child's memories can help paint a fuller picture of what it was like growing up with the parent and the family. Their knowledge and recollections can aid in constructing a more complete understanding of the parent's life and character. They offer perspectives on the family's medical history, cultural heritage, and personal. The insights a raising child can provide is invaluable, particularly when the genetic parent has passed away.

When someone reaches out to their genetic parent's raising child, the person may be excited at the prospect of a new sibling, may feel jealousy, and may not really know how to navigate the flood of emotions that accompany such a discovery. They may experience an emotional whirlwind, ranging from intrigue about their parent's past to a protective hesitation over the family dynamic they've known. Their view of their parent and familial relationships may change with knowledge of how the new sibling was conceived.

This encounter can redefine relationships and requires sensitivity and openness from both sides. As new siblings forge a path forward, it's crucial to acknowledge the complexity of feelings that might arise. A dialogue between the newly connected siblings can pave the way for a broader family narrative, enriched by multiple perspectives and shared experiences as well a gateway to connection to the family for the newcomer. Over time, these relationships can mature into a beautiful kinship.

R

raising (social, adoptive, supporting) parent

...is the person who raised you, who is legally responsible for you, and may or may not be genetically related to you.

Our protagonist discovers the joys, challenges, and unpredictable moments of raising a child in a unique family dynamic. Similar to "Instructions Not Included", they must navigate the complexities of their child having multiple parents in an unscripted adventure, highlighting the resilience and creativity inherent in parenting. "Parenting Unscripted" is a tribute to the love and support children receive from their raising parents who help them navigate the messy and emotionally challenging journey of life. This tale reassures us that in the world of parenting, the most reliable guide is the heartfelt bond shared between parent and child.

Parenting Unscripted (Instructions Not Included)

Raising (recipient, social, supporting, or adoptive) parents, play a pivotal role in the lives of their children. They are the figures present for a child's key moments in life. They may not share a genetic connection with their child, but their love and support embody the true essence of parenthood.

Many children grow up in unique family arrangements. This often means that a child may have multiple parents in their life. When someone refers to a "step," "raising," or "genetic" parent, there is no inherent negative or positive connotation. These terms simply help to clarify which parent they are talking about. There are many different terms used to mean a raising parent. These include:

- Adoptive Parents (AP), including Adoptive Mothers (AM) and Adoptive Fathers (AF), who legally adopt a child.
- Recipient or Intended Parents (RP) are those who become parents through third-party reproduction.
- Father that Raised Me (FRM) and Mother that Raised Me (MRM).

Raising parents, in their varied forms, significantly impact the development of their children, on emotional, psychological, and epigenetic levels. They provide more than physical care—they contribute to emotional, moral, and psychological growth. The bond between a raising parent and a child is a powerful testament to the diverse and profound nature of family connections, transcending genetic ties and highlighting the impact of love, commitment, and shared experiences.

We have the capacity to love multiple parents. The search for genetic parents by some individuals is not a reflection of the love or quality of care provided by their raising parents. It's driven by the natural desire to understand one's origins. During this potentially turbulent quest for identity and familial information, the support of raising parents becomes more vital than ever. They provide invaluable guidance and emotional backing, helping navigate the complexities of searching, possible reunions, or the challenge of facing rejection. Their role during this period underscores the enduring strength and significance of the bond shared with their child.

People should be permitted to refer to their parents in whatever fashion makes them conformable; this may change over time.

ℛ
real parent

...is someone who provides unconditional love, guidance, and support; who fosters their child's growth and well-being, regardless of genetic ties.

Based on the "The Pursuit of Happyness", this narrative highlights a parent's unwavering commitment, akin to Chris Gardner's devotion to his son. "Endless Love, Limitless Support" shows that being a real parent can transcend genetics and is defined by infinite love, steadfast support, and the dedication made to their child's wellbeing. This story celebrates the journey of parenting in all its forms, demonstrating that the heart of a real parent is measured not by blood, but by the love, guidance, and resilience they provide in the unwavering pursuit of their child's happiness and success.

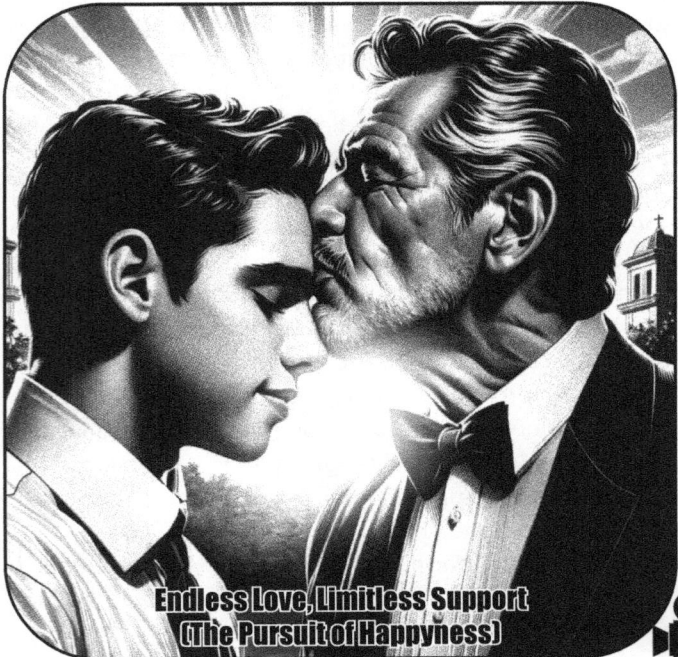

Endless Love, Limitless Support
(The Pursuit of Happyness)

The term 'real parent' is multifaceted and can carry different meanings depending on the context in which it is used. Sometimes when someone refers to their "real parent," they might be alluding to a genetic connection. In other cases, they could be acknowledging the person who provided care and support throughout their upbringing. This term, however, can be emotionally challenging for a raising parent, especially if they are not genetically related to their child, as it may feel like a negation of their parenting efforts.

A real parent, whether they are a raising parent, a genetic parent, or someone who embodies both roles, is defined by their child-centered approach. They act in the best interest of their child, providing a loving, safe, and nurturing environment. This involves practicing empathetic and consistent communication and maintaining truth and transparency at age-appropriate levels. They offer guidance, discipline, care, and support, nurturing their child's growth and development.

The love and concern of a real parent for their child are unconditional and lifelong. They understand that their primary role is to help their child blossom into a well-adjusted, functioning member of society. Being a parent is a lifelong commitment, where the journey involves supporting their child through life's complexities, including the exploration of genetic origins.

A real parent understands that love is not finite and that family dynamics are inclusive, not exclusive: family is AND not OR. The search for genetic parents by their child does not diminish the years of experiences, love, and support shared. In fact, a real parent understands that supporting their child in this experience can further strengthen their bond. They know that the essence of parenting lies not just in the genetic link but in the shared journey of life, the moments of care, understanding, and unconditional support.

This broader and more inclusive definition of a real parent acknowledges the diversity and complexity of family relationships in today's world, celebrating the profound impact of nurturing, regardless of genetic ties.

Each person should be permitted to use 'real parent' however they wish for whichever type of parent they want and their use may change over time.

R

right to know

...is a principle asserting that individuals have a right to know information about their personal identity, heritage, parentage, and genetic origin from birth.

In "The Kids Are Alright", it is a fundamental right to know one's genetic identity just like the right to love and marry whomever you want. No revelations needed from a DNA testing kit. This tale weaves the emotional journey of children and parents alike, as they navigate the complex web of genetic connections and familial bonds. The real treasure here is the knowledge of one's genetic identity. In this take two, there's no need to confront ethical dilemmas and the reality of genetic connections because this time the kids know who their genetic parents are from birth. This story reveals how to navigate complex modern families.

The Kids Know & It's Alright (The Kids Are Alright)

The 'right to know', a concept steeped in the principles of human rights and personal identity, stands at the intersection of ethics, law, family dynamics, and emotional well-being. It affirms the fundamental right to be aware of one's genetic identity and from birth, and its profound implications for individual health, psychological development, and cultural belonging.

The right to know extends to critical aspects of personhood and existence. It encompasses access to medical history, which can be crucial in preempting genetic diseases or conditions and informing healthcare decisions. It plays a role in the formation of self-identity, providing the missing pieces for those who have felt disconnected or different from their raising family. It connects individuals to their heritage, offering a sense of continuity and belonging. And, it enables relationships with genetic relatives, preventing inadvertent close-relative romantic relationships.

International frameworks like the U.N. Convention on the Rights of the Child, which has been ratified by every country but the U.S., emphasize the child's best interest as a primary consideration and explicitly acknowledges the right of a child to know their parents and maintain their identity. This includes preserving and providing access to information about one's origins. These concepts are further echoed by the Hague Conventions on Inter-country adoption.

In the U.S. the legal landscape is fragmented due to states having authority over family law, resulting in a patchwork of regulations that affect the extent to which individuals can access information about their genetic identity. There's a need for federal legislation (like seat belt requirements or the national drinking age) to pressure states to enact a common legal framework that provides access to genetic identity and heritable medical and mental health information for all adults.

Advocates argue that this right is not just about satisfying curiosity but about fulfilling a deeper biological and psychological need. It's about the integrity of the self, the understanding of one's place in the continuity of generations, and the potential to prevent significant health issues. The call for the right to know is a call for truth and transparency, recognition, and respect for the individual's need for a coherent narrative of their own life.

S

secrets fester

...is the physical, psychological, and emotional toll that the act of holding a secret can exert on an individual's well-being and relationships.

In "Veiled Truths", secrets weave a complex tapestry in the Arnold household. Behind closed doors, a festering truth about their children's genetic origins strains the seams of their family life. As the family navigates the veneer of suburban perfection in their 'true lies', the concealed truth lurks, threatening to unravel the trust and love they've built. It's a tale of emotional espionage where the hidden costs are counted in silent struggles and broken bonds. When the secret comes to light, they must confront the reality: the truth doesn't just sting—it transforms. It is the telling of a secret that is the key to freeing ourselves from the prison we didn't know we built.

Veiled Truths (True Lies)

The act of concealing a child's true genetic origins is a profound secret that can lead to deep-seated emotional, psychological, and relational issues. Keeping a secret like this is akin to experiencing trauma and can set off the body's alarm system, notably the amygdala, inducing a state of perpetual alertness and emotional reactivity.

Keeping such foundational information secret is often under the guise of protection, stemming from a belief that ignorance is bliss or due to cognitive dissonance. However, this decision sets the stage for a complex web of consequences. The emotional toll on the secret holder, burdened by the weight of their continuous deception, can manifest in numerous ways, including stress, anxiety, and guilt as well as physical illness. These feelings can strain their interactions with the child, often leading to overprotectiveness, detachment, or inexplicable tension.

For the child, the revelation of such a secret, often unearthed inadvertently or through a life event necessitating genetic information, like a medical emergency, can be earth-shattering. It can lead to feelings of betrayal, loss of trust, and questioning of one's identity and family bonds. The foundation upon which they understood their place in the world is upended, leading to potential estrangement and a reevaluation of familial relationships. The parent-adult child relationship can be irreparably harmed.

The relational dynamics within the family unit and extended family can suffer while the secret is held. After the secret's revelation, it often brings to light not just the concealed information but also the underlying reasons for the secrecy. It can uncover further family secrets such as infertility, infidelity, or other life circumstances that led to withholding the truth, as well as other unresolved conflicts, compounding the emotional fallout.

A significant family secret does not merely fester and lie dormant, it actively undermines the fabric of trust and connection that binds a family. Secrets usually have a way of coming out, especially with DTC DNA testing. While this may provide some answers, it often also raises more questions. Healing from such a revelation requires time, openness, and, most importantly, a willingness to rebuild trust and understanding from all parties involved.

S

sibling

...is someone with whom you develop a deep familial bond, characterized by shared experiences, mutual support, and a profound emotional connection, whether through genetic ties, adoption, or life circumstances.

Just like in "The Family Stone", the focus of this film is a large, eclectic family gathering, but with a twist. The story weaves the lives of siblings connected through various means: some are step-siblings, two are linked through the same sperm donor, and a one just discovered a new genetic sibling after an NPE. This narrative explores the challenges and joys of accepting and embracing these diverse sibling relationships, and the ultimate realization that family bonds are built on more than just DNA, but that DNA can be a place to start.

Tangled Roots: The Family Stone Redefined
(The Family Stone)

113

In the intricate tapestry of family dynamics, the term sibling encompasses a wide range of relationships, each unique yet equally significant in the hearts of those involved. While the nuances of these connections may vary, the essence of siblinghood remains constant—a bond characterized by shared experiences, emotional support, and an enduring connection.

Stepsiblings are children brought together by the union of their parents. Though not related by blood, these siblings often form bonds just as strong as those shared by genetic siblings, navigating the complexities of a blended family together.

Brother Raised With (BRW) and **Sister Raised With (SRW)** refer to siblings with whom one shares a childhood, only to later discover they are half-brothers or half-sisters. This revelation may redefine the relationship but doesn't diminish the depth of the bond forged over years of shared experiences.

Cross Siblings occur in families where each parent brings children from previous relationships, creating a network of half-siblings who are connected through one shared parent.

Dibblings are siblings from donor-conceived families. They share a genetic connection through a sperm or egg donor but are raised in different families (this term is disliked by some DCP). These connections can be just as strong as any other sibling relationship.

Full Siblings share both genetic parents and may or may not be raised together.

Newly Discovered Brother/Sister (NDB/NDS) are siblings discovered later in life due to various circumstances, such as adoption, an undisclosed affair, or sperm/egg/embryo donation. These discoveries can lead to new, meaningful relationships, and an expanded sense of family.

Sibling by Choice is a powerful testament to the fact that familial bonds are not confined to genetics. These are individuals not related by blood but who choose to form a sibling-like bond, often as strong and profound as any genetic connection.

Siblings play an integral role in shaping one's identity and life experience. They are companions in the journey of life, sharing joys, sorrows, and the countless little moments that define family. The diversity in sibling relationships reflects the evolving nature of family, proving the heart of siblinghood lies in mutual care, shared memories, and the unspoken promise of being there for each other, regardless of how the relationship is created.

_S_

synchronicity

...is a similarity between previously unknown close genetic relatives that reveals shared traits, mannerisms, and preferences.

Echoing "August Rush", imagine a symphony of life where the manifestations of the melody of genetics is known. This film explores the synchronistic genetic connections between relatives. It's not just the notes that are perfectly aligned but their very DNA, revealing the profound ways DNA presents in common speech patterns, liking the same color, disliking the same foods, professional preferences—even among close genetic relatives that did not grow up together. As the story unfolds, each new relative strikes a chord, resonating with the idea that our talents and traits are more than just coincidences; they're echoes of our ancestry.

Echoes of Ancestry (August Rush)

Synchronicity, a term coined by psychologist Carl Jung, refers to the meaningful coincidences that occur in our lives, which seem too significant to be the result of mere chance. In the realm of misattributed parentage, late discovery donor conceived (LDDCP), late discovery adoption (LDA), non-paternal events (NPE), and DNA surprises, synchronicity takes on a very real role. Individuals who uncover their genetic roots often report uncanny similarities with their newly found relatives—commonalities in preferences, mannerisms, speech patterns, temperaments, and even life paths—that defy explanation by environment alone.

These shared traits, extending to likes and dislikes in colors, food, music, and career paths, suggest an underlying genetic script playing out across generations. Robert Plomin, a renowned behavioral geneticist and psychologist, provides a data-backed narrative to these anecdotal observations. With decades of research, Plomin's work indicates that DNA does indeed matter, more than we had once assumed, more than your environment you are raised in. Read about his research in *Blueprint: How DNA Makes Us Who We Are*.

Heritability helps us understand this phenomenon. It doesn't predict individual outcomes but explains variations within populations. For example, 80% heritability of height means most differences in height among people can be linked to DNA. Around 50% of psychological traits are due to genetics. This interplay is further nuanced by the concept of the nature of nurture: our genetic predispositions influence the environments we select for ourselves. While our environment can impact us, their effects are often transient. The concept of hedonic adaptation, as demonstrated in the 1978 study by Brickman et al. entitled *Lottery Winners and Accident Victims: Is Happiness Relative?* shows that people tend to return to a baseline level of happiness regardless of major life events (regardless of whether these events are 'positive' or 'negative").

In the context of family and parenting, these insights are transformative. While parents matter immensely in the formative years, their influence on personality, mental health, or cognitive abilities appears to wane over time. What remains constant is the genetic undercurrent that subtly guides individual propensities. As such, it's crucial for parents to nurture their children's innate interests and talents, working with the genetic grain rather than against it.

Synchronicity in genetic discoveries highlights this beautifully—revealing that while we forge our paths, there's a hidden map written in our DNA that resonates with those who share it, often leading to a profound sense of coming home, of finding a piece of ourselves in close genetic relatives that we never knew was missing. These meaningful coincidences in family resemblances and shared idiosyncrasies are just a reflection of our genetics and strengthen the bond between genetic relatives and enrich our understanding of identity and belonging.

RESOURCES
People with an NPE

FACEBOOK GROUPS
- Adoptees, NPEs, Donor Conceived & Other Genetic Identity Seekers
- Cross Cultural Connections from a DNA Surprise or MPE
- DNA NPE Friends
- DNA Surprise Support for MPE Family & Friends
- DNA Surprises Support Group
- DNAngels NPE/MPE DC Search & Support
- MPE Jewish Identity and DNA Surprises
- MPE Life: DNA Surprise, NPE, Adoptee, & Donor Conceived (DCP)

NPE FRIENDS FELLOWSHIP

DOCUMENTARIES
- Doubting Thomas
- Little White Lie
- Stories We Tell

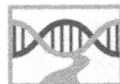

UNTANGLING Our Roots

DNA Surprise Retreat

CONFERENCE & RETREATS
- DNA Surprise Retreat: NPEs, DCP, & Adoptees
- Untangling Our Roots: Annual Conference

PODCASTS/AUDIO
- CutOff Genes
- DNA Surprises
- Everything's Relative
- Family Secrets
- Family Twist
- Missing Pieces - NPE Life
- NPE Stories
- Sex, Lies & the Truth
- The Bradley Hall Show
- Weird & Surprising Facts

CHILDREN'S BOOKS
- *A Family Is a Family Is a Family*, Sara O'Leary
- *Where Is My Dad?*, Ambry L Ivy & Taylor Ivy.
- *I Didn't Leave Because of You*, Tyechia White
- *Families Come in Many Forms*, Bella Mei Wong
- Families, Families, Families, *Suzanne Lang*
- *From the Start*, Stephanie Levich & Alana Weiss
- *It's NOT the Stork! A Book about Girls, Boys, Babies, Bodies, Families, and Friends*, Robie H. Harris
- *The Family Book*, Todd Parr

Not Parent Expected
CANADA

DNA Search Help

- DNAngels

BOOKS FOR ADULTS

- *A Broken Tree: How DNA Exposed a Family's Secrets*, Stephen F Anderson
- *Ancestry Discoveries*, Annette L Becklund
- *Black Lotus*, Sil Lai Abrams
- *Exposed by DNA*, KS Hopkins
- *Finding My Roots: A Journal of Discovery & Reunification*, DNAngels
- *Folksong: A Ballad of Death, Discovery, and DNA*, Cory Goodrich
- *How DNA Testing Is Upending Who We Are: The Lost Family*, Libby Copeland
- *I Had My Underwear on the Entire Time*, Michael and Amy Blair
- *Junkyard Girl: A Memoir of Ancestry, Family Secrets, and Second Chances*, Carlyn Montes De Oca
- *My Re-Birthday Book: This is My Story for adoptees, donor conceived, and people with an NPE, who are misattributed, or who've had a DNA surprise*, Kara Rubinstein Deyerin JD
- *My Surprise Family: Find Your Ancestry Story*, Margaret M. Nicholson, PhD
- *NPE: A Story Guide for Unexpected DNA Discoveries*, Leeanne R. Hay
- *Raceless*, Georgina Lawton
- *The Dark Little One*, Shirley Munoz Newson
- *The Milkman's Son*, Randy Lindsay
- *The Stranger in My Genes*, Bill Griffeth
- *The Survivors: A Story of War, Inheritance, and Healing*, Adam P Frankel
- *White Like Her*, Gail Lukasik
- *Who Am I?: Identity in the Age of Consumer DNA Testing*, Dr. Anita Foeman and Bessie Lee Lawton, Dr. Anita Foeman
- *Who Even Am I Anymore:* Eve Sturges, LMFT
- *Who's My Daddy: A Tale of DNA Surprises and Discovery*, Joel Gottfried

Severance
ON THE AFTERMATH OF SEPARATION

WATERSHED
D N A

DNAngels
Finding Families, One DNA Strand at a Time

323-TALK MPE
RIGHT TO KNOW
www.RightToKnow.us

DONOR CONCEIVED

FACEBOOK GROUPS

- Adoptees, NPEs, Donor Conceived & Other Genetic Identity Seekers
- Anonymous US
- DNA for the Donor Conceived
- DNA Identity Surprise & This MPE Life
- Donor Children
- Donor Conceived Offspring, Donors, Parents
- Donor Sibling Registry
- Friends of Donor Conceived Individuals
- Gen Z Donor Conceived People
- International Donor Offspring Alliance
- We Are Donor Conceived
- Worldwide Donor Conceived People Network

DOCUMENTARIES/FILMS

- Anonymous Father's Day
- Baby God
- Donor Unknown
- Father Mother Donor Child
- Filling in the Blanks
- Offspring
- Our Father
- Missed Conceptions
- Sperm Donors Anonymous

PARENTING BOOKS

- *Three Makes Baby*, Jana Rupnow

CONFERENCES & RETREATS

- DNA Surprise Retreat: NPEs, DCP, & Adoptees
- Untangling Our Roots: Conference

BOOKS FOR ADULTS

- *Brave New Humans*, Sarah Dingle
- *Chosen Family*, Kiara Rae Schuh
- *Experiences of Donor Conception: Parents, Offspring & Donors through the Years*, Caroline Lorbach
- *Finding My Roots: A Journal of Discovery & Reunification*, DNAngels
- *Go Ask Your Father: One Man's Obsession with Finding His Origins Through DNA Testing*, Lennard Davis
- *Inheritance: A Memoir of Genealogy, Paternity, and Love*, Dani Shapiro
- *My Re-Birthday Book: This is My Story*, Kara Rubinstein Deyerin
- *Normal Family: On Truth, Love, and How I Met My 35 Siblings*, Chrysta Bilton

- *Relative Strangers: Family Life, Genes, and Donor Conception*, Peter Nordqvist and Carol Smart
- *Scattered Seeds*, Jacqueline Mroz
- *The Genius Factory*, David Plotz
- *The Ones We Choose*, Julie Clark
- *The Right to Know One's Origins: Assisted Human Reproduction and The Best Interests of Children*, Juliet Guichon, et al.
- *Thicker than Water*, Kerry Washington
- *Triple Helix*, Lauren Burns
- *Uprooted*, Peter J. Boni
- *Who Am I: Experiences of Donor Conception*, Dr. Alexina McWhinnie

CHILDREN'S BOOKS
- *And Tango Makes Three*, by Justin Richardson
- *Building My Family: A Story of Egg Donation & Surrogacy*, Carrie Eichberg, Psy.D.
- *Extra*, Kaeleigh MacDonald
- *Families Come in Many Forms*, Bella Mei Wong
- *From the Start*, Stephanie Levich & Alana Weiss
- *Hope and Will Have a Baby: The Gift of Egg Donation*, Irene Celcer
- *It's NOT the Stork! A Book about Girls, Boys, Babies, Bodies, Families, and Friends*, Robie H. Harris
- *Little Treasure*, Anat Georgy
- *Meeting My Brother*, Jennifer L. Dukoff
- *My Extra Special Leaves*, Jean Wrights
- *Our Story: How We Became A Family Series*, Nina Barnsley and Stephanie Clarkson
- *Ready-Made Sweetie: All Mixed Up*, Whitney Williams
- *Sophia's Broken Crayons: A Story of Surrogacy from a Young Child's Perspective*, Crystal Falk
- *The Chicken Who Couldn't Lay Eggs*, Sabine-Julie De Brus
- *Telling and Talking Booklets*, UK DC Network
- *Training Wheels; How Did I Get Here*, Chris Barrett and Sally B. Hunter
- *What Makes A Baby*, by Cory Silverberg
- *Zach's Safari: A Story about Donor Conceived Kids of Two-Mom Families*, Christy Tyner

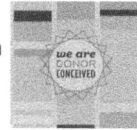

PODCASTS/AUDIO
- BioHacked
- Go Ask Your Father
- Half of Us (Half of Me)
- Insemination
- Luke, Who is Your Father?
- Message in a Bottle
- Three Makes Baby
- You Look Like Me

ADOPTEE

FACEBOOK GROUPS
- Adopted Adults Support Group
- Adoptees in Search of Their Birth Family
- Adoptees Only
- Adoptees Only: Found/Reunion The Next Chapter
- Adoptees Supporting Adoptees
- Adoptees, NPEs, Donor Conceived & Other Genetic Identity Seekers
- Adoption Healing Network
- Adoption Reunion Search and Support Group
- Adoption Search & Support by DNAngels
- Adult Adoptees of Color
- Adult Adoptees Support Group
- Cross Cultural Connections from a DNA Surprise
- DNA Adoptee Research & Reunion
- DNA NPE Friends
- DNA Surprises Support Group
- DNAngels Search & Support – NPE/DC
- Find Birth Parents, Siblings, Adoptees and Family
- Korean Adoptees
- MPE Jewish Identity & DNA Surprises
- MPE Life: DNA Surprise, NPE, Adoptee, & Donor Conceived
- The Adoptee in Me

NAAP
NATIONAL ASSOCIATION
OF ADOPTEES & PARENTS
EDUCATE · ELEVATE · EMPOWER

WATERSHED
D N A

UNTANGLING
Our Roots

CONFERENCE & RETREATS
- Adoption Initiative Conference - St. John's University
- Adoption Knowledge Affiliates Conference
- Against Child Trafficking Symposium
- Alliance for the Study of Adoption and Culture Conference
- Celia Center Los Angeles Virtual Adoption Symposium
- Concerned United Birthparents Retreat
- DNA Surprise Retreat: NPEs, DCPs, & Adoptees
- Korean Adoptee Adoptive Family Conference
- Male Adoptee/Alumni Impact Summit
- National Association of Adoptees and Parents Mini Retreats
- Rudd Adoption Research Conference
- Untangling Our Roots Summit

DOCUMENTARIES

- @ghostkingdom
- Adopted: for the Life of Me
- Blank
- Calcutta is My Mother
- Closure
- Dan Rather Presents: Unwanted in America
- Father Unknown
- Lion
- Open Secret
- Philomena
- Reckoning with The Primal Wound
- Secrets & Lies
- Six Word Adoption Memoir Project
- The Girl in the Picture
- The Good Adoptee
- The Lost Child
- The Other Mother: A Moment of Truth
- Three Identical Strangers
- Twinsters
- You Follow: A Search for One's Past

PODCASTS/AUDIO

- Adapted Podcast
- Adoptees On
- Adoption Advocacy
- Adoption Unfiltered
- Black to the Beginning
- Born in June, Raised in April
- Conversations About Adoption
- Dear Adoption
- Jigsaw Queensland
- Luke, Who is Your Father?
- The Adoptee Next Door
- Who Am I Really
- Once Upon a Time In Adopteeland

Saving Our Sisters

ORGANIZATIONS

- Adoptee Rights Coalition
- Adoptees Connect
- Adoption Knowledge Affiliates
- Adoption Mosaic
- Adoption Network Cleveland
- Adoption Search Resource Connection (ASRC)

CTTA

Good Policy for Everyone.

- Celia Center
- Coalition for Truth & Transparency in Adoption (CTTA)
- Concerned United Birthparents (CUB)
- DNAngels
- Male Adoptees
- National Association of Adoptees & Parents
- Right to Know
- Saving Our Sisters
- Watershed DNA

Concerned
United Birthparents

ADOPTIVE PARENT & KINSHIP CARE
- Adoptive and Foster Family Coalition NY
- Adoptive Parents Committee
- Aptitude: A Support Group for Adoptive Parents Facing Adoption's Challenges
- Center for Adoption Support and Education
- Encompass Adoptees
- I am adopted
- Kinship Caregiver Virtual Support Group
- National Center on Adoption and Permanency
- The Honestly Adoption Company
- DVD Series: Adoptive Parent Training

ADOPTION
MOSAIC

CHILDREN'S BOOKS
- *Adoption Is Both*, Elena S Hall
- *I've Loved You Since Forever*, Juliette C. Bond
- *Sam's Sister*, Juliette C. Bond
- *Surrounded by Love: An Open Adoption Story (Open Adoption Stories)*, Allison Olson
- *Tell Me Again About the Night I was Born*, Jamie Lee Curtis
- *The Story of My Open Adoption: A Storybook for Children Adopted at Birth*, Leah Campbell

MIDDLE AGE BOOKS
- *For Black Girls Like Me*, Mariama J. Lockington
- *See No Color*, Shannon Gibney
- *The How and The Why*, Cynthia Hand
- *The Inexplicable Logic of My Life*, Benjamin Alire Sáenz
- *The King of Slippery Falls*, Sid Hite
- *The Length of a String*, Elissa Brent Weissman

ADOPTION
KNOWLEDGE
AFFILIATES

BOOKS FOR ADULT ADOPTEES

- *A Fire is Coming*, Emma Stevens
- *Adoption Unfiltered: Revelations from Adoptees, Birth Parents, Adoptive Parents, and Allies*, Sara Easterly, Kelsey Vander Vliet Ranyard, and Lori Holden
- *Austerlitz*, W.G. Sebald
- *Akin to the Truth / After the Truth*, Paige Strickland
- *All You Can Ever Know*, Nicole Chung
- *American Baby*, Gabrielle Glaser
- *Birthmark*, Loraine Dusky
- *Coming Home to Self: The Adopted Children Grows Up*, Nancy Verrier
- *Finding Karen Black: Roots Become Wings*, Diane Bay
- *Forbidden Roots*, Fred Nicora
- *Growing Up Black in White*, Kevin Hofmann
- *Hole in My Heart*, Loraine Dusky
- *I'll Always Carry You: A Mother's Story of Adoption*, Linda Franklin
- *In Their Own Voices: Transracial Adoptees Tell Their Stories*, Rita J. Simon and Rhonda M. Roorda
- *My Re-Birthday Book: This is My Story*, Kara Rubinstein Deyerin
- *No Names to be Given*, Julia Brewer Daily
- *Parallel Universes: The Story of Rebirth*, David Bohl
- *Recycled*, Jack F Rocco MD
- *Second Choice: Growing Up Adopted*, Robert Andersen
- *Tapioca Fire*, Suzanne Gilbert and Michelle Kriegman
- *Thank God I Was Adopted: Cause DNA is No Joke!*, Pekitta Tynes
- *The Child Catchers*, Kathryn Joyce
- *The Family of Adoption*, Dr. Joyce Maguire Pavao
- *The Girls Who Went Away*, Ann Fessler
- *The Goodbye Baby: Adoptee Diaries*, Elaine Pinkerton
- *The Lies That Bind*, Laureen Pittman
- *The Other Mother*, Carol Schaefer
- **The Primal Wound, Nancy Verrier**
- *The Truth So Far*, Jennifer Dyan Ghoston
- *Uprooted*, Peter J. Boni
- *You Don't Know How Lucky You Are*, Rudy Owens
- *You Don't Look Adopted*, Anne Hefron
- *You Should Be Grateful*, Angela Tucker
- *You'll Forget This Ever Happened*, Laura Engel
- *Who Am I Really*, Damon Davis
- *Why Be Happy When You Can Be Normal?*, Jeanette Winterson

It is a fundamental human **RIGHT TO KNOW** your genetic identity

www.RightToKnow.us / info@RightToKnow.us

www.ingramcontent.com/pod-product-compliance
Lightning Source LLC
Chambersburg PA
CBHW021832020426
42334CB00014B/592